Georgia de Chamberet was born i[...] and an artistic mother. She spent a [...] between England and France, attending various schools in the UK and a lycée in Paris. In the 1980s she worked at Quartet Books in London as managing editor for the Quartet Encounters paperback series and published contemporary European writers in translation, including Denis Belloc, Annie Ernaux, Juan Goytisolo, Hervé Guibert, Alexandre Jardin, Tahar Ben Jelloun, Daniel Pennac and Gisèle Pineau. She left the company in the 1990s to found her own literary agency, BookBlast Ltd. She lives and works in Notting Hill.

From the reviews for *XCiTés*:

'*XCiTés* is a collection of French writing in translation by a new generation which aims to smash the stereotypes. Illustrating France's struggle to be pluralist, this book is an interesting insight into exactly where French culture currently stands . . . From the dinner guest who despises the ignorance and complacency of her friends as they quote haikus at each other over the brie in Marie Desplechin's "Haiku" to the hugely evocative and disturbing tale of a woman's urge to scratch off her own skin in Lorette Nobécourt's "Irritation", the majority of these writers seem caught up in the vacuum of their suffocating bourgeois backgrounds. Without the usual class stratifications, the bourgeoisie have nothing to fight against but the sense of what it is to be French . . . Writers from other cultures or from the gay scene provide fresh air: Mounsi's tale of losing his immigrant father to poverty and alcoholism and Abdourahman Waberi's account of addiction and madness in an African shanty town – these ring with a sense of truth and a lack of self-consciousness ... *XCiTés* shows that the next generation of French writers are tackling the stagnancy of their culture head-on. They're sending out signals that France could be much more than a place where the croissants are heaven and great things used to happen.'   *Sunday Glasgow Herald*

'Georgia de Chamberet has collected together a diverse, often exceptional band of young writers, with distinctive voices and coming from a wide variety of backgrounds: Paris, the old colonial empire, *France profonde*, the seedy and the sexually charged ... The translations are uniformly and exceptionally good, often pyrotechnical in their virtuosity. In the end, even Camus might have been impressed by the *audace*. Sex, drugs, rock and roll, *and* style!'   *London Magazine*

'*XCiTés* brings together, in a rare and welcome move, first translations of new French fiction. In a stream-of-consciousness, Guillaume Dustan's narrator tries for a gay encounter, but everyone involved is too stoned; 'trance' is the background music and general flavour of Mehdi Belhaj Kacem's story, "Anteform"; in Frédéric Beigbeder's story, "Trashed", people are popping 'euphoria' and drinking 'lobotomies on the rocks'. In the sex stories, even the desire is acidic: Virginie Despentes's heroines are rabid, spewing sex addicts; the narrator in Michel Houellebecq's coolly cruel story makes himself sick in a nightclub before masturbating ... Much more organic is the other social aspect, the one which reflects the changing ethnic face of France – the writers of African origin . . . Perhaps the best stories are the ones which aren't part of any of this: Vincent Ravalec's "Black-Magic Nostalgia" is a brilliantly understated combination of eeriness and humour, and Houellebecq has an extraordinary voice.'

Gaby Wood, *Observer* Paperback of the Week

'This collection of stories, features and works-in-progress from the next generation of Edgy Young Things, bristles with aggression and energy. Drugs, clubs, murder – it's all fuel for the cold, aimless rage that drives many of these powerful stories.'

Carrie O'Grady, *Guardian*

'Goes right to the heart of current French obsessions – alienation in the *banlieue*, the Front National, the new music scene and football.' Lucy Dallas, *TLS*

'The insularism of British publishers and readers is perhaps unsurpassed. The result is an entire generation of European authors who go untranslated, unpublished, unnoticed here, who have not yet made the breakthrough into public consciousness of, say, Günter Grass or Italo Calvino. Certain publishers, however, are havens of enlightenment . . . *XCiTés* is a useful introduction to the more go-getting young Gallic authors.'

Catherine Lockerbie, *Scotsman*

'An eclectic mix of fiction, film and individual testimony, showcasing the movers and shakers of the French scene . . . A sharp and penetrating insight into the fin de vingtième siècle.' *Flux*

'These short stories from the French new wave fly in the face of racists to celebrate France's multi-cultural reality. Pressure meets rebellion and resistance. The perfect Eurostar read.'

Straight No Chaser

'Is French literature finally waking up? There are increasing signs that a new generation of writers has emerged, with new energy, new subjects, and a new take on life in the information age. So, where should you turn to sample this new dynamic in French literature? A good place to start is *XCiTés* . . . Georgia de Chamberet has put together translations of the work of 15 French authors, all under 40 and unpublished in English . . . The writing is strong and it's refreshing to read so much good fiction set in a real-life Paris, with the smell of the metro late at night, the CRS on the street corners and boring dinner parties in the 16th with hostesses called Anne-Lise . . . The writer everyone is talking about is Michel Houellebecq, a novelist and essayist who has been hailed as the most important new French voice in a long time.'

Paris Free Voice

'The self-appointed guardians of *la belle* France's literary culture are currently undergoing one of their endemic spasms of horror at the state of contemporary French writing. The emergence in print of a polyglot, multi-racial, disaffected youth culture – a generation of Gallic Irvine Welshes – has rather ruffled their *savoir faire*. In a way, you can understand their fears. For if, as they contend, the barbarians are indeed at the gate, French litera-ture has more jewels than most to lose. Few other countries can claim a tradition as strong as the one bequeathed by the likes of Voltaire, Flaubert, Hugo, Zola, Balzac, and, for those seeking light relief, Dumas *père et fils* ... If you quite like barbarians, [however], you could always try *XCiTés*, a new anthology of contemporary French writers ....'

Glasgow Herald

'Now that Paris has reclaimed its title as the centre of youth culture it seems as good a time as any for Georgia de Chamberet to collect together some of the chic-est young things to come out of France since Jean-Luc Godard hung up his black polo neck ... With films like the excellent La Haine seemingly being made on an annual basis in France, a World Cup-winning side infiltrating our Premier League, and Antoine de Caunes all over the TV, this book captures the very zeitgeist of modern European culture.'

Lincolnshire Today

'Phew, quel scorcher! This is a collection of new French writing which suggests the French have a very curious outlook on life and love. But you knew that, didn't you? Liberated language, liberated attitudes, a lot of violence and a great deal of sex ... Carrying *XCiTés* in Cannes should generate major beach-cred.'

Bristol Evening Post

XCiTés

the Flamingo Book of New French Writing

edited and with a preface by
Georgia de Chamberet

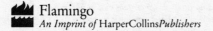
Flamingo
An Imprint of HarperCollinsPublishers

Flamingo
An Imprint of HarperCollins*Publishers*
77–85 Fulham Palace Road,
Hammersmith, London W6 8JB

Flamingo is a registered trade mark of
HarperCollins*Publishers* Limited

www.**fireandwater**.com

Published by Flamingo 2000
1 3 5 7 9 8 6 4 2

First published in Great Britain by
Flamingo 1999

This book is supported by the French Ministry for Foreign Affairs,
as part of the Burgess Programme headed for the French Embassy
in London by the Institut Français du Royaume Uni

institut français

ISBN 0 00 655191 2

Set in PostScript Plantin by
Rowland Phototypesetting Ltd,
Bury St Edmunds, Suffolk

Printed and bound in Great Britain by
Clays Ltd, St Ives plc

Acknowledgements

with thanks and peace and happiness to Christov Rühn, Olivier Poivre d'Arvor, Geraldine d'Amico, Roger Palmer, *Les Inrockuptibles*, the British and French publishers, the contributors, the translators, BookBlast authors and friends and so many others . . . for their support of and belief in this passionate roller-coaster of a book

Contents

Preface

Georgia de Chamberet

Chelsea Football Club's training ground, Hatton Cross, Middlesex. I'm waiting to interview Marcel Desailly, one of the key players of the '98 World Cup-winning French team. A memorable encounter. The drive and the vision behind his words reflect, in many ways, the real France of today.

One of the most powerful countries at the heart of Europe, France considers itself to be the birthplace of ideas and politics, of refined sensual living, and the guardian of a language to be preserved and revered. The *idea* of France is a potent one – which thrives beyond its shores. But forget those glorified clichés to which so many Francophile pundits and tour-promoters cling: cafés and Left-Bank existentialism, sultry sexy sirens and pouting starlets, Godard and Truffaut, Coco Chanel and chic little poodles, châteaux and fine wines, Provence and pastis, brie and baguettes, Magnum Photographers and Robert Capa's Generation X, Duras and *le nouveau roman*, 1968 and all that . . .

Being a cultural hybrid gives you a special perspective. It enriches you; enables you to see from the inside and from the outside. I set out to revisit my birthland under an independent light. To question perceptions of France and the French. To overthrow stereotypes or even create new ones! To discover writers, cultural catalysts, whose stories, experiences and forms of expression are so strong they transcend cultural and national boundaries – are universal. To showcase the best translators –

linguistic *passeurs*. Realising *XCiTés* has been a revelation, an odyssey. The book gradually assumed its own passionate momentum and identity.

France is going through a period of apocalyptic change and growth, reflected in the cultural explosion of the last two decades. It is gradually beginning to *accept* rather than *deny* that it is a cultural mosaic of attitudes, faiths, languages and traditions, and to recognise the voice and power of its suburbs and inner cities. Herein lies its strength and its future. French society is on the move. Underground club culture has gone global, as the melodies of Air, DaftPunk and MC Solaar permeate the world. The '98 World Cup victory established it as a major footballing super-power. Cult movies such as *Betty Blue* and *La haine* set precedents for international film-makers. And its great theorists are toppling from their pedestals . . .

XCiTés captures the radical, creative spirit of the '80s and '90s driving France into the millennium and beyond. It offers a vision of a country, a society, in transition, through the writing and ideas of inimitable individuals working outside and inside France's frontiers. *XCiTés* features specially commissioned contributions from Marcel Desailly, champion world-class defender and hero of youth and Christov Rühn a.k.a. DJ Tov, anarchic visionary at the heart of underground club culture – now mainstreamed. Their pieces complement a selection of stories and extracts from novels by an entire generation of new and disparate authors (at commission, under the age of forty and unpublished in the UK and the US), whose books have, in many cases, become runaway bestsellers not only in France, but across the European mainland. The raging debates stimulated by these writers is a good sign, since innovation invariably provokes negative criticism, and positive support. Balzac and Flaubert, Sagan and Camus, Perec and Genet, Chamoiseau and Cardinal, are as representative of their times as are the young authors in this anthology, and generally provoked just as much outrage and debate in their day.

'The old dream, The Novel, has never died' (Tom Wolfe). The writers selected for *XCiTés* have a powerful style, language, vision and humour all their own. Certain great French writers have had an effect on their work, while others have prompted irritation and disgust by their cold cerebrality and self-indulgent navel-gazing (Sartre and the exponents of *le nouveau roman* in particular). They are storytellers, entertainers, linguistic experimentalists; some have a wicked and at times subversive sense of humour (a quality featuring more and more in French writing). All represent a major departure from the past, an opening up of new horizons inside France, embracing a lateral worldview. Excitement, the city, XTC, regeneration X: Les XCiTés.

Virginie Despentes is the ultimate kick-ass fuck-the-system anarcho-babe. Marie Desplechin and Agnès Desarthe portray the more well-heeled *milieux* of Parisian life in which men and women of all ages dysfunction with style. Tonino Benacquista is the no. 1 true-grit voice of the realist new wave of crime writers

Preface

and TV-culture satirists. Guillaume Dustan charts the uppers and downers of gay night and day life. Frédéric Beigbeder laughs at and with the glitzy, trashy fun and dark side of *le chic et branché* Tout Paris clubbing. Ilan Duran Cohen is the Woody Allen of French literature. Vincent Ravalec shows the modern Rastignac as a sure-fire, charming crook. Mehdi Belhaj Kacem, philosopher of misfits, the chemical generation and XS, creates an intricate philosophy of endurance through destruction. Lorette Nobécourt is unique in the way she expresses her torment through a body raging against barriers and social norms. Abdourahman Waberi is *the* poetic lance of the younger post-colonial writers whose roots stretch back into the African continent. Mounsi, the child of immigrants brought into France as a source of cheap labour (all of whom were dumped in the inner cities), is the real thing, as opposed to those frauds manufactured by publishers for commercial gain. Michel Houellebecq is one of the founders of and contributors to the magazine *Perpendiculaire*, and the catalyst of a pioneering group originally hailed by the French media as the most exciting *mouvement littéraire* since *le nouveau roman*. Recently rejected by his circle for being so outrageously politically incorrect, he made front-page news across the national press yet again. Eric Faye's writing, evolving from the classic *essai philosophique-littéraire*, has a strong politico-human twist laced with fantastical-magical realism. Mathieu Lindon, reclusive polemicist and powerful journalist-provocateur, is currently 'outing', through fiction, the extreme right-wing, racist politicians at the root of nationwide irritable gut syndrome. Mathieu Kassovitz's *La haine* remains unbeatable in its depiction of urban unrest and the pain-fuelled hate of inner-city kids. Based on an improvised film script and featuring vivid slang, parallels can be drawn with Gary Oldman's conception and scripting of *Nil By Mouth* which was filmed inside a South London estate.

Britain's Gallic neighbours aren't quite what the Brits think they are. They are boldly reinventing themselves, crossing a threshold . . . and are perhaps a little less different after all.

Georgia de Chamberet

April 1999

Marie Desplechin

Haiku

I **arrived late, intending to melt** discreetly into the crowd, knowing everybody would already be well tanked-up. As predicted, they were all there, sloshed, Anne-Lise perched brazenly on Jean-Marc's thigh, showing off in front of his advertising friends.

Sitting buttock to buttock on the sofa in front of the coffee table, Daniel and his companion Darian were the only ones not wearing jackets. They were all talking loudly, and the braying of their voices formed a canopy over the dense cloud of cigarette smoke. When I walked in, the company nodded a greeting. Daniel was the only person to smile at me, and I picked my way through the mob to squeeze in next to him. There was no room on the sofa, so I sat down on the rug at his feet.

'How are you, sweetie?' he asked, bending down towards me.

Then, without waiting for a reply, he whispered in my ear:

'Watch it, they're even more excruciating than usual!'

Daniel meant Anne-Lise's friends. I glanced around the room. I had already come across most of the individuals gathered for the evening. Young men with smug faces, young women wearing lashings of make-up who acted as if they were being paid to laugh loudly across a bowl of peanuts. Interrupting each other continually, repeating the same scraps of phrases again and again, exclaiming in feigned surprise, they spun out endless anecdotes devoid of any content. From time to time, the din was broken by an intermission of painful silence, which Anne-Lise took it upon herself to break with a shrill laugh or an injunction to the circle of friends: 'You'll never guess who . . .' she'd venture desperately.

I should never have accepted this invitation. I knew I'd be bored out of my mind for hours, a whole chunk of time when I could have been reading quietly at home, stretched out beside my cat.

I couldn't even rely on Daniel to salvage the evening. We had found ourselves sitting next to each other at the same dinner parties so many times, we didn't have much left to say to each other. We kept our major confessions for the rare occasions when the two of us were alone. But it's not enough to enjoy each other's company in private to inject conversation into a trendy soirée.

Daniel, one hand on Darian's knee, at least had the comfort of not being alone. Darian, silent and smiling, certainly seemed to be profoundly bored. But he was always like that. Darien barely spoke a word of French. So he was probably used to being there, without expecting or hoping for any more than Daniel's loving presence, and a hand on his knee. I envied the pair of them, protected by their love and their coupledom. I felt horribly alone. Isolated at the end of the sofa, we were drinking in silence when Anne-Lise, tearing herself away from the ricocheting conversation, realised that not everyone had been introduced.

'Christiane!' she cried, 'Daniel! I don't think you know Martine or her friend Bruno.'

There was every reason not to know them. Nor did we particularly want to. We were introduced by force.

'Where did she find those two?' I asked Daniel when our names had been exchanged to our mutual indifference.

'I know the girl. Anne-Lise has already mentioned her to me. She's a sales assistant. I think her parents are Korean. When Anne-Lise was looking for extras for the Badedas shoot, she got in touch with them. Believe it or not, they agreed to do it. I don't know about him. I bet he's an officer in the sales battalion, that he plays tennis and listens to Barry White. In any case, I'd be very surprised if he wandered up and down the beach in a sarong, selling chips, or did late night gigs in bars.

There we were, bitching in a whisper, when we had to go and sit at the table. The evening may have been a disaster, but there was one good thing about it, time was passing. We could rely on the fact that it would eventually end, and that after coffee, everyone could go home. All we had to do was wait.

I plonked myself at the end of the table, next to Daniel, who was firmly parked next to Darian, on whose knee he placed his hand. Oh my God, that enviable strength gays have, of togetherness, even when they're alone. And how painful heterosexuality and its inescapable solitude is, even when you are with someone.

Anne-Lise had excelled herself, from the inevitable tomato and mozzarella salad to the no less conventional pasta. We formed a lively, stylish gathering. The talk turned to sports –

where they played and the best equipment. Tennis, squash and golf, for starters. Oh puh-lease. I was morose and silent, a non-entity. I sat there, at my end of the table, insipid and almost ugly. I was so aware of my non-existence that I didn't even care about myself any more. For I was certain of one thing: nobody could see me, nobody would remember me.

I took the opportunity to stare unashamedly at the men sitting round the table. Taken as a group, they were big and stupid, reared on cereals, with tans cultivated on the beaches of Brittany. Beneath the day-to-day tiredness, an elastic, well-rounded, bourgeois material was discernible. By evening, most of them had a five o'clock shadow, a hoarse voice and a little sports car parked recklessly outside the building. How cosy to have one of them at home for evenings and weekends. How lovely to watch him sorting out his gear, rackets and clubs, car keys and well-cut jackets. Lovely to listen to him describing the brute force required to win the hostile soap, tyre or yoghurt market. Lovely, finally, to feel the weight of his great, stupid body lying on top of yours and to touch, in a conjugal torpor, his rugged, familiar skin.

Which one? I wondered. But, faced with the choice, I found myself put off each time by a chin that was too heavy, a neck that was too fleshy, or a voice that was too thick. Impassive, I was quietly musing as the conversation turned towards food. Anne-Lise was bringing a huge piece of runny brie to the table.

★　　★　　★

With hindsight, I can only put the little drama that then erupted down to the brie, and the wine. Jean-Marc was ostentatiously opening some more Bordeaux when Anne-Lise suddenly decided to change the subject so as to hog the limelight.

'Do any of you,' she asked point-blank, 'know about Haikus?'

Jean-Marc smiled modestly beside her. I kept quiet. My throat tightened with apprehension and disgust.

'I do,' whispered tiny Martine, who until then had been hiding in the shadow of huge Bruno, confining herself to fluttering her eyelids at regular intervals. 'I do, they're little Chinese poems.'

'Japanese!' screeched Anne-Lise. 'Japanese!'

'Yes, of course, Japanese,' murmured Martine, retracting her delicate face into her tiny shoulders.

'Listen to this,' proclaimed Anne-Lise:

> *the ancient pond*
> *a frog leaps in*
> *the sound of water*

Not really surprised, I felt a slight disappointment. So, Anne-Lise hadn't judged it necessary to expand her knowledge since we had last seen each other.

'The Haiku is much more than a little poem,' she declared in a voice full of tannin. 'It's a whole philosophy.'

I myself must have had quite a bit to drink. For, heedless of the consequences, I butted in unceremoniously from my end of the table.

'No, not a philosophy,' I thundered, 'it's a whole way of life.'

Turning to look at me, Anne-Lise glared.

'Philosophy, way of life, it's all the same,' she yelled across the plates.

I was about to retort when, to my consternation, tiny Martine took advantage of the brief moment of silence to draw attention to herself once more.

'Yes,' she whispered, shooting me a murderous sideways glance. 'I agree completely with Anne-Lise, absolutely. Because . . .'

Everyone had stopped talking, gobsmacked by the novelty of the subject and by the sudden violence of the exchange. Turning away from Anne-Lise for a moment, Jean-Marc gazed at Martine full of emotion.

'Yes?' he said, inviting her to go on, amid the general hush.

'Because it's Zen,' she stammered, in the voice of a prepubescent ant, 'it's dead Zen.'

This time, the gathering turned towards her as one. She stared at them with the same mesmerised look. As if every single one of those fools, taking themselves for Pinto, was discovering Japan in person. And she, with all those masculine eyes on her, putting on an air guaranteed authentic. An absolutely authentic air. And to think she's Korean. May her ancestors forgive her, it pains me for their spirits.

'Haikus,' she went on with a cajoling smile, fulfilling everyone's expectations, 'Haikus . . .' she went on, and her voice dropped directly into her boots.

That's all. It was over. She retracted her neck with a very graceful swanlike movement. For a few minutes, the guests observed a Delphic silence. Then, seeing that they would not get any more out of her than a panic-stricken smile only partially veiled by her hair, they gave up.

'Fascinating,' muttered Jean-Marc. 'What did you say your name was?'

'Martine,' she murmured into the ashtray.

The hubbub had started up again. I kept quiet, staring into my greasy plate. I had so much hatred in me that I couldn't move. I was afraid it would spill out.

Cutting the brie into generous portions, Anne-Lise pretended to ignore me. I furtively glowered at her. Just then, there was a ring at the door.

'At last,' said Anne-Lise. 'Oliver . . .'

She got up awkwardly from the table and went to open the door, teetering on her infinitely long legs. She returned, dragging behind her a man who really stood out from her collection of athletic, foodie friends. First of all, he was short. Secondly, he wasn't wearing a jacket. Lastly, and above all, he was black.

Black-skinned. That took the biscuit. Because after all, you don't find many black friends in our circles. Once again, our amazed crowd fell silent. Bravo Anne-Lise. If she wanted to entertain her friends this evening, she had certainly pulled it off.

'Typical Anne-Lise, following the latest fad,' commented Bruno, seemingly meaning the Haiku, but pointedly referring to this latest arrival.

'Hello,' said Oliver, without being offended by our sceptical interest.

He must have been used to being in the minority.

'Don't move. I'll grab a chair and sit at the end of the table. I was just dropping by for coffee.'

'Let me introduce Oliver,' raved Anne-Lise triumphantly, running her hand through the perfect square of her blonde hair.

Then she turned to me.

'I met Oliver on the Sabena account,' she told me curtly. 'He also works for Mondial Fabrique from time to time. You're sort of colleagues. You work for the same people . . .'

Disaster. She'd invited him for me. Or at least, that's what she was going to pretend now. But what was I supposed to do with this dark guy blown in by the night? I tried to protect myself, with desperate bad faith.

'That doesn't mean a thing. We probably don't work in the same department. Or on the same floor. And I don't know all the copywriters.'

In vain. Oliver was indeed trying to squeeze a chair in between Daniel and me. He sat down and smiled at me amiably. He had a round face, fine, regular features and his skin was the colour of cloves. Without the shadow of a doubt, this guy's roots reached back to the Indian sub-continent.

'Pleased to meet you,' I finally conceded once he was seated, but I didn't extend my hand.

He smiled again, bowing his head.

'I'm a translator. I've worked for you several times. We might have bumped into each other.'

'Oh no. No, most definitely not. I don't know everybody at Mondial. In fact I'm rather cut off in my office.'

From a distance, Anne-Lise was keeping a wary eye on me.

'Then this is a chance to get to know each other,' he ventured, amid the exchanges that were being resumed around the table.

'Hmm,' I said.

She was clearly trying to lumber me with the first immigrant she'd been able to find. But why the hell did she have to interfere with my life? She'd do better to keep her eyes on her photographer who was zooming in on the exotic Martine's face, in close-up. Why?

A basket of mandarins and lychees replaced the brie and I kept ferociously quiet. I deliberately ignored my black neighbour, who, elbows on the table, was pretending to listen to the disjointed conversation that was somehow being maintained around the room. Daniel and Darian, enclosed in their bubble of affection, whispered to each other, laughing. I champed at the bit when I distinctly heard Anne-Lise's voice rising once again above the contours of the meal.

'Oh no,' she squealed. 'Nothing like French poetry . . . it's must less, how can I describe it . . . much less elaborate. We have completely different sensibilities, you see. Japan and Europe, I'm not saying it's a question of civilisation, but I mean, there's no comparison.'

She was showing off shamelessly. She had gone too far. She deserved a thrashing. Incensed, I banged my fist on the table.

'You really are talking complete nonsense,' I cried, to drown the sound of her voice. 'And not only do you not know the first thing about it, but you're talking disgusting crap. If you had used your brain for a moment, you'd see that Apollinaire can easily be compared with Natsume Soseki, to name but two.'

'Hey, Christiane,' cut in Jean-Marc banging both hands on his knees. 'You're not going to make a scene over a bunch of foreign writers who've been dead for centuries. We haven't even heard of these guys. It's not worth it.'

'More fool you,' I retorted. 'Shut up. I'm telling you it is worth it. I prefer to argue over a Basho who's been dead for four centuries than over a dickhead like you. And you Anne-Lise, listen to this, and compare:

Marie Desplechin

The sky is of copper
no glimmer of light
The moon seems dead . . .

'Well?' said Anne-Lise open-mouthed, as Jean-Marc dozed off, his head slumping into his lychees.

'Well, it's Verlaine, would you believe?'

'What about Verlaine?'

'Nothing,' I replied despondently. 'It was a comparison. But it's pointless. You haven't got a clue.'

I shut up, exhausted. She must have sensed the contempt beneath my weariness, for suddenly, she lost her rag.

'Stop getting so uptight,' she screamed, 'you're ruining my dinner party.'

Then she called upon the entire company as a witness.

'Christiane, who's so clever, is going to recite us a genuine French Haiku. Go on, Christiane, go on, share a little of your knowledge with us, if you don't mind.'

I didn't mind. I got to my feet, looked at them, and said:

Bunch of idiots
Screw the whole damn lot of you
I'm pissing off home.

'Goodbye,' I added, leaving the table.

'Goodbye,' chorused Daniel and Darian, who were the only ones to laugh.

'Goodbye,' said the short brown man, looking up at me with curious round eyes.

The others watched me leave in silence. I slammed the door as hard as I could behind me.

The next day, I was roused by the telephone ringing.

'Hello? Hello?' grated Anne-Lise's voice.

'Oh shit!' I said to my cat, and nearly hung up.

But she didn't give me a chance. She went on the offensive.

'Are you completely off your rocker, or what? Why on earth did you get so uptight? Jean-Marc thinks you need help. And Martine thinks you're horrible.'

'Great,' I said. 'Who's Martine anyway?'

'The Chinese girl who was there yesterday.'

'Oh, come on, Anne-Lise, she's Korean.'

'Same thing. Do you realise you screwed up my dinner party? How do you think it makes me look?'

Suffocating under this avalanche of reproaches, I didn't answer.

'Oliver left without saying a word about you. But you can be certain that you won't see him again. That's the last time I invite a guy for you. The last time. Because I invited him for you, I did,' she insisted bitterly.

'You invited him for me? But he's into guys, isn't he?' I retorted. 'That takes a weight off my mind. I stupidly worried all night that I'd missed out on the last heterosexual in Paris who you hadn't had between the sheets.'

'Me? Had between the sheets? A black guy?' squawked Anne-Lise.

I banged the phone down. Dammit, she got on my nerves.

Virginie Despentes

Fuck Me

Huge, rather chic brasserie. Waiters in black-and-white outfits. Both at the bar, perched on high stools, in front of glasses of cognac ridiculously large for the shots. Manu is wearing a dress so short it looks like she's not wearing anything when she's sitting. Up to the bush and her blouse revealing one of those multi-coloured bras she's famous for.

They kept an eye out on the way, but didn't pass a single young or doable guy.

A chubby, balding bloke, wearing a blue suit, sits next to them. Bovine smile. Manu gives Nadine an inquisitive glance, she answers:

'I can't decide: it'd really be immoral, but it'd really be immoral. In the end, I'm up for it.'

Manu leans over to him as he speaks to her. Complains about the heat, widens the opening of her blouse to cool off, big time. He compliments her on her smile. Libidinous. He wipes his neck often because he's sweating like a fat pig. He's breathing heavily, smiling at them dumbly, unaware he's baring yellowed, stained teeth. Clumsy, moronic, grotesque, and he's showing off bravely. Must definitely think they're idiots to dare try his luck. Or else doesn't have a clue, really.

Sordid puns and fleshy grimaces. He's so pathetic he becomes almost likeable, just a matter of shifting perspectives.

He has hot flushes as soon as Manu brushes up against him. And she doesn't really brush up, she sticks to him, has him feel her belly, moves a thigh against the cloth of his suit, and shows her underwear any which way she can.

She doesn't handle booze lightly, and she's clearly excited by his repulsiveness and by rubbing up against him.

Nadine plays cute and lowers her eyes when he first grabs her by the waist. Since she acts more demure and less tart-like than her pal, he goes for her first.

Manu's looking on, asks the man to pay another round, and while he's busy attracting the attention of the waiter, declares:

'Anyway, the dumber you are, the better it works. It took me a while to actually believe it . . .'

Nadine sighs, shrugs and says:

'You got to see it their way. There's no way they can perceive things as they are.'

Since the bloke has managed to place the order, he wants to get back into the conversation. He tries, jovial:

'What's it you're saying, girls?'

Manu's staring at him, anything but sweet, and barks:

'You and your breath stink!'

The man thinks he's misunderstood, or missed something. Nadine is laughing. Manu takes him by the arm and says cheerfully:

'You look like an open-minded guy; so me and my friend, we're not going to beat around the bush for long. We're looking for an understanding partner, we go to a hotel, we screw nice and sweet, then that's it. Any chance?'

Nadine grabs his other arm, explains very gently:

'If you don't mind, love, let's fuck instead of talking, we're more likely to get along that way.'

He stutters then chuckles like a tempted virgin, except at the corners of his mouth he has near-dried white drool. Mouth snot. Her approach troubles him enormously. He has to make an effort to collect his thoughts.

In any case, he hasn't made the link between them and the two girls in the news. He hesitates between several emotions: he's triumphant because he's going to screw both of them and he's the filthy type and without enough dosh to visit the pros. He's a bit unsettled because they're too up-front. So much served up on a plate is fishy. He chooses to see it as his lucky day. He's a tad disappointed too, because it would have been better if he had had to do his schmooze-act, to feel like he'd forced them a bit. But he tells himself nothing's perfect.

He doesn't mind at all that they look a bit odd; all he takes in is that they are girls. And that he's going to screw the two.

He pays for the hotel room. He claims they are his nieces to the pink Polish woman at reception, who couldn't care less and barely listens. Because he's nonetheless ashamed that all three of them are going to do it together. Manu and Nadine watch him without saying a word, slightly dismayed.

In the lift, he gropes Manu with small, brusque movements, as if to make sure it's all for real and that she won't protest. Or even pretend to. The excitement sears his neurons and swells his nostrils. He's inflamed; not a pretty sight. His eyes bulge and his hands are out of control, he looks possessed, in a trance. He's one of those guys who can't behave themselves when they're over-excited. Nadine looks at him as he pants and swallows, his eyes popping out of their sockets. Girls don't ever get excited like that just thinking about doing it. It makes her feel a little desire, and simultaneously, a little disgust.

Manu allows herself to be touched up, obligingly, without returning a single stroke, but she enjoys feeling him do it and seeing him in such a state.

When the lift stops, she says:

'Shit, they really sweat in this heat, he's all sticky, the fat fool.'

Addressing Nadine. So disconcertingly natural that he doesn't respond. He seems to be thinking about something else.

Nadine looks at Manu's hand on the blue fabric. Beneath, the outline of the growing prick. Growing as much as it can, that is. And she's looking at the fingers running along the zip. The wrist going up and down convincingly. The man's hand fondling the breasts vigorously. The little one arches up so he can caress her all he wants.

The hotel room is decorated in orange flowered wallpaper. That makes it seem familiar, like all other cheap hotel rooms. The wallpaper is peeling off in places, the pink bedcover is stained with brown blotches.

Standing in front of the man, Manu undresses, her eyes

fixed on him, he never looks at her face. Her movements are mechanical and smooth, with the exaggerated sensuality of a pro. Not much conviction needed for the required effect. He is literally mesmerised.

Leaning against the wall, Nadine watches them attentively.

The man pulls Manu to him, buries his big face in her belly, licks her eagerly calling her 'my little flower'. He's holding her by the waist, a thick bracelet glitters on his wrist, his fingers are slightly hairy. His square nails dig in her flesh. He spreads her lips with his nose and burrows in.

For a while, the little one looks at him as from a distance, stroking his head pensively. As if surprised to find him there and sorry to be unable to enjoy any of it. And, at that point, she's not angry with him, she doesn't despise him.

Nadine is masturbating softly, against the seam of her jeans, doesn't take her eyes off the hands nervously running over Manu.

The little one moves away from him slowly, leans against the edge of the bedside table. Grabs her thighs and spreads them wide apart. Painted nails on inside thighs play around her hole. Then insist and enter. She turns around without stopping, moves a finger from anus to vulva. Sideways, she's looking at Nadine who's slid down the wall, now crouching. Neither is smiling, they're doing something serious and important. They're not thinking about anything in particular.

The man is still seated, his eyes open wide. He searches his pockets, takes out a condom, stands up and comes up behind

Manu. Before penetrating her, he begins to cover his organ. Manu turns round and grabs his wrist:

'Just your cock. Nothing on it.'

He tries to explain that she's missed the point. That it's stupid, even for her, to do it unprotected. She moves again him, back first, rubs her arse up and down him. He resists weakly, lets himself be rubbed and protests, unconvinced. Begins to fondle her arse repeating that's how he wants to take her, shoot his wad.

With no warning, Manu goes to sit. She says:

'Your dick's soft. I'm sick of it.'

She takes a bottle of whisky out of her bag, has a swig, hands it to Nadine. Then she lights a fag. The bloke is beginning to find their weirdness unpleasant. He considers clearing out, but his libido won't let him: such a lucky break!

He sits next to her and suggests timidly, but he's ready to insist:

'I don't know what's happening. Maybe you could ... Maybe with your mouth?'

He's got it into his head that he could get sucked without a condom. He thinks he's pretty smart for that one.

'You're lucky I'm a dedicated girl and with a taste for a job well done. Can't say I don't feel like kicking you out.'

And without flinching, she takes him in her mouth and works him vigorously. The man looks at Nadine for a bit of moral support. He's got it in his head that she is nicer than the little one and he's expecting something from her.

She's looking at him unkindly. Something's over-exaggerated in him, too deep in stupidity.

Manu is kneeling between his legs. She's blowing him conscientiously, and mechanically strokes the inside of his thighs. He says: 'That's good, you see, it's coming' while playing with her hair. Then holds her tighter and sticks it deep in her throat. She tries to get away, but he's holding her down and wants to bang her tonsils with his knob. She pukes between his legs.

Rolling on their backs in seconds, it takes them a good minute to stop laughing.

He's at the sink, washing himself, infuriated.

They're dying of laughter, seeing him so angry. He loses it:

'I can't see what's so funny. You're so . . .'

He's searching for his words as they repeat, chant-like: 'choked on something', and the phrase is a big hit.

Now, he's losing it in his corner, full on, and calls them fucking degenerate whores while putting on his clothes, enraged. As he's about to leave, Manu stops laughing and blocks his way:

'Fucking degenerate whores is well put and perfectly correct. But you weren't the one to come up with that one, wanker. And nobody's told you to go.'

He protests that they hadn't told him he'd have to pay, that he doesn't have any money on him and that, at any rate, she's got a nerve to ask for money after what she's done. Manu smashes her fist in his face, as hard as she can, yelling in a low voice. Her face is deformed by rage, her mouth twisted by tension when she speaks to him, but she's careful not to make too much noise:

'Did I say anything about money?'

He doesn't react. He wasn't expecting her to hit him. He doesn't seem to cope with violence very well, he looks paralysed. He doesn't even protect his face and doesn't try to defend himself. Nadine whacks him on the side of the head with the bedside lamp. She lets out a loud sigh when she hits him, like a tennis player. He stumbles, Manu goes for the jugular and knocks him to the ground. She's not half his weight, but she's going at it so hard, she can handle him. She sits across him, grabs his throat. When he begins to scream, Nadine pulls at a blanket, covers his face, and sits on it. The body is moving, but they're in a tight clench. Manu whispers:

'Mister, what we didn't like about you was the condom. Your fatal mistake was the condom. You're found out, geezer, you're just a condom-wearing wanker. You shouldn't go around following chicks you don't know, mister. That too, you had to understand. You've got to watch out. Because in this case, you know who you've met, mister? Fucking killers of condom-wearing-wankers.'

Convulsions. With a hand he beats frantically at the floor. Maybe he'd done judo as a kid and the gesture is some sort of reflex. Useless.

Nadine is on her feet and kicks him frenziedly, the way she saw Fatima do it to the cop's head. The more she kicks, the harder she kicks, she senses bits are breaking, now and then. Soon, she can feel her thigh muscles working.

They go at it together until he's completely motionless under their blows.

They're drenched and breathless when they stop. Manu lifts a corner of the blanket, makes a disgusted grimace and gets up.

In his jacket, they find a bit of cash.

Side by side, they're washing their hands, putting on eye-liner. They're giggling, nervously repeating: 'choked on something' and 'condom-wearing wanker'.

Leaving the hotel, nobody says anything. They've been as quiet as could be.

Nadine insists they take the train.

In the street, they can't stop laughing, Nadine's back starts to hurt and she has to pause to catch her breath. Manu shakes her head:

'Fucking hell, I can't believe it. That wanker thought I'd swallow all his cum, and I puked on his cock. Tough shit. Wrong place, wrong time . . .'

Tonino Benacquista

The Bad Boys' Garden

———

It was seven in the morning when I met this revolver. When I say 'met', that's the word. I had the impression of making an acquaintance. I decided to take it in my hand, to see if I was capable of it, find out what you felt at that moment. It started in my palm, like a shiver that ran up my forearm, fast. I clenched my fist as tight as possible. I couldn't stop myself from play-acting, drawing the gun ten times from an imaginary holster. Then I took aim, with my arm extended, not trying to pull the trigger. Fear of the weapon, I suppose, and of the noise it might make.

For months my childhood friend José had been begging me to dig out that school photo, taken thirty years ago, with the pair of us grinning in the front row, next to the teacher, sitting on the dining-hall bench. I ransacked the cellar where Grandma – known in the family as Malou – stowed everything away. But in the midst of all that junk I couldn't find my satchel and exercise books.

A yellowing tablecloth caught my attention, its four corners knotted together as if ready for a journey. It was the first time I had seen this bundle, even though it had always been there in fact, right under our noses, except that children only ever notice what matters to them. And what kind of mystery could this table-cloth be hiding, when your quest was for the wooden horse with the broken leg, or Stack Shop storage boxes crammed with photos and a few old sugared almonds? Knots once jerked tight fell loose at once. My memory dredged up Malou's expression, now that as a grown-up I'd finally discovered what she'd always kept hidden from us inside that faded cloth.

— a Mauser;

— an Italian army .34;

— a sawn-off shotgun (with its cartridge clip nestling in a missal hollowed out to hold it);

— a USM 1 carbine;

— an automatic rifle, with 'Eugénie' carved on the stock;

— a loaded Colt revolver.

And a list of the arms cache scrawled on the cover of an unused notebook, which I read out loud ten times running, just to hear the marvellous rasp of the names. You only have to say 'Colt' and you've changed. You become one of those who walk on the other side of the street.

As I stroked the Mauser, I wondered whether the trigger where my index finger rested hadn't felt the touch of other more lethal fingers – fingers that could kill. Whether this gun had been pointed at a stranger ready to fall, and if this sight had been targeted on a head, a heart, or a piece of fence.

No one, not even my late father, knew the source of those weapons, unless shame had kept him silent all those years. He spoke to us about Malou with that insidious respect whose aim above all is to create distance. Maybe, as a kid, he too had untied those knots. Who'll ever know?

I look at my watch. It's nearly ten o'clock at night. I am convinced that my own story, the true story of my life, began this morning at seven o'clock, at the very moment when I stroked the Colt and span the cylinder.

Today I didn't go to work.

I took a day off, something I've always longed to do. To stray from my usual path, walk the streets as someone else, drift where I never usually go. To go out to play. A stowaway in my own life. It's obvious that the Colt gave me the opportunity. To roam the streets with a revolver in working order, all day long, was seizing the chance to be somebody else. I felt it by the tingling in the hollow of my hand when I pretended to shoot. Straight away, from the very first touch, ideas crossed my mind, things I'd never thought of. Never.

Where do you aim, to be certain of killing? To immobilise? To cause suffering for a while before the final shot?

How do you act when the police are after you? Do you keep count of the bullets you fire?

Do you hide the gun in your overcoat pocket? Your jacket pocket? Or stick it in your waistband, for reasons of secrecy and speed?

I felt like a killer, then a victim, then a cop, then a gangster, saw my own film with me in every role. I even created the part of Malou, a poor woman worn down by the Occupation, searching the grey-green uniform of a soldier lying dead beneath an apple tree, and wrapping up the equipment in a family tablecloth, as if to exorcise that evil metal.

I chose the Colt. I swore not to remove it from my pocket, no matter what happened that day.

As I slipped through the drizzle that promised sunshine in the afternoon, I realised at once that I hadn't been mistaken.

That drunken thrill, from the very first step.

Take the third turning left, down the street I never use because it no longer leads anywhere or to anything in particular. Tipsy I felt, just a touch intoxicated, just from walking in the street. That's all, a walk in the street. In any case I couldn't fail to notice that I wasn't walking the way I normally do, that my back was unusually straight, my head relaxed, taking care that nothing showed, neither the bulge of my fist, clamped round the butt of the gun, nor the strange feeling of impunity that might betray my gaze at any second.

I'd almost forgotten the street-name, Hollowtree Street, but I still remembered the snack bar run by a woman whose bad temper José and I would risk just for the sake of pinching coconut balls from her sweet rack. I assumed she'd been dead for years, but it was she who served me that cup of coffee around half-past eight. At one table I saw two old men, the retired glazier and the ironmonger. It's as if the people who've been old for as long as you remember never die.

With a trace of a smile, the owner called me little sticky-fingers, asked for news of that other little thieving tearaway, and apologised for not having come to Malou's funeral. At the sound of her name, the glazier rose to his feet and jeered. His Alsatian stood up with a bristling growl, loyal to the hostile reflex of its master who didn't try to pacify the dog, but if anything encouraged it by making hostile gestures. What could Malou possibly have done to stir up so bitter a memory, years after her death? I had no time to wonder, because the dog was agitated, it was snarling and ready to bite, and the old man too was growling in my direction. It was then that I took fright. I tightened my grip, and started to draw the gun, my finger on the trigger.

And I saw, in a dream, the dog: its skull blown apart by a bullet fired at point-blank range. Because you have to kill dogs that bite because of the madness in their owner, you have to kill them, despite their innocence, despite their love, you have to kill them, exterminate them, despite their having been made into monsters.

The dog sensed something – in that way dogs are sharper than humans. It actually flattened itself on the floor in front of me, whimpering, as if to beg my forgiveness. It knew.

Hollowtree Street leads to a stretch of wasteland that I trod like a jungle, jumping back and forth between mats of brambles and rutted mud. Long ago I used to play there, with José and the rest of the gang. The bad boys' garden. With the passing years, this dump has lost none of its sorry reputation. The first syringes to be used in the neighbourhood were found there. Hooligans were picked up there after various street brawls. Then there was the case of the rape that shocked the city: a girl found dead, two years ago now. The case of the 'rape in the bad boys' garden', as the local paper called it. I've always kept well clear of that patch of ground. Fear, superstition, rumour, I don't know what else. But that morning, around nine o'clock, in the last shades of night, I prowled there like a conqueror.

I soon found myself back in the city-centre, which was already buzzing. All around I spied ladies, shopping bags, market stalls. The city, the low-rise council estate, the town hall. Surprised by it all – the general bustle and morning smile on some of the passing faces, the sun emerging earlier than expected. Going past a row of suburban houses, I stopped outside the one that belongs to that shit Étienne, at the time when he's usually swilling down the day's first litre of red. I peered through the window, to make out his awkward shape behind the curtains. Already hunched over, already feeling ill.

No one would have seen me go in, or come out. No one would have suspected a visit, or anything. I could just have chucked the Colt down a drain, and no one could have guessed that it came from inside Malou's tablecloth, most likely salvaged from the tunic of some dead American, sprawling not far from his parachute. No one at work would have noticed that I'd come in a bit late. No one would cry for Étienne.

I wondered if life was offering me a replay, just one. An erratum from the past. One pencil stroke. One slight correction of fate. That morning I was sure that it was. I took a last glance through the misted window pane, to gaze at Étienne, as stooped and sick as ever. I took a deep breath, like a lungful of serenity regained. And went on my way.

I ate at the wrong time and walked in the wrong direction. Alone at last. A tourist amused by his own daily routine. In the distance I saw my colleagues emerge from the office and flock to the café over the road for the day's special.

My son always worries me when he talks about the chip stall on the edge of town. It didn't take much to find it. So this was where he hung out, munching those greasy sausages, showing off his jacket studded with trashy stars, playing the young rebel to impress his fiancée. The group of kids there no doubt wondered what this old tosser could be up to, knocking about on their territory, but they suddenly lost interest in me when a 504 estate jammed on its brakes in front of them, overturning a moped at their feet. Some men got out, real ones, tough nuts, with slim ties, long overcoats and leather gloves – more than a match for trainers and threadbare Levis. Ordinarily I would have walked away, to spare myself macho theatricals, because after all no one is obliged to live on greasy chips or shake arrogant hands. But not this time.

The kids were too frightened to move. One apologised and cringed like the glazier's dog, another took out some money to pay for I don't know what, and a third just stood there as his moped was flung into the middle of the road. I didn't give a moment's thought to my own brat, the one who could have been there. One of the four bad boys stared me in the eye and advised me to piss off. He was the one I slapped first, a glorious slap, a side-to-side one-two one-two, the way they do in films, and with my left hand, because my right hand, slick with sweat, still gripped the warm gun metal. After a moment's consternation I slapped a second one, smiling. How I'd have loved them to react, to flip out. Their fear enraged me more and more; I shouted, lashed out with my feet and fists, let rip, to shake them out of their unbearable dumb stupor. But all I heard was the slam of car doors and the roar of the gunned engine. The kids took me for a hero. My son could have been there among them, gawping at me too. In fact no greater coward had ever set foot on the scene.

The rest of the day was eventful. I lived through a series of 'first-evers'. The first bar where I threw a glass at the neat ranks of bottles, the first cop whose eye I held till he looked down, the first descent to the underworld down the shadiest street in the roughest district I could find. It all went much better than I could have imagined as I spanned a range of unknown feelings – arrogance, cynicism, contempt – but I had time to right some wrongs, issue one or two challenges, and indulge in a few magnanimous gestures. It was enough just to want it, to override my goodwill, to look for the edge, and see it recede and recede, and be powerless to reach it. That is what pained me most, without a doubt.

* * *

I didn't go home. Around eight o'clock that night I returned to the bad boys' garden, where, safe in some kid's den, I am trying to put down on paper every last detail of this crazy day. So that something remains. I mustn't forget a thing, especially from the start of the morning. The memory of that tingling in the palm of my hand, those shivers. Then that drunken feeling. Mustn't forget to write about that drunken feeling, just from walking in the street – from the very first steps. How do I talk about that intoxication, express it? I have to say, too, that around mid-afternoon I wondered whether I didn't have a real knack for carrying a revolver. Or if I had the makings of a killer. It seems to me that the answer was no. I just wanted to be somebody else, and had I been able to predict that it would work out so well, no doubt I would never have embarked on the experiment. I must note down everything. You don't carry a Colt without paying a price. It was good to feel it melt in to my hand. How do I talk about that? I'm a normal person. I fear the precariousness of things and people. I didn't want to go home, so that it would last a bit longer. I enjoyed being that other man. Because he is me, after all. And I've tried to say it with ordinary words. And what about tomorrow? Would I have had to walk down the street as if nothing had happened? Tomorrow I'll know no more about the mystery of Malou; no doubt I'll never know what she did to the glazier. Tomorrow Étienne will still be alive; continuing to pay in drink for what he did to me. José still won't have his photo. My son will hear the story of the unknown enforcer of justice who roughed up some bad boys. My colleagues will make a dash for the day's special. And all the people I met will remember me tomorrow, and maybe the day after.

I've stopped writing for a moment to check the cylinder one last time. And I've wiped the muzzle of the gun, to avoid the tang of rust in my mouth.

Michel Houellebecq

The Port of Call

_____

Ah yes, to have values!

When I got back to La Roche-sur-Yon I bought a steak knife in Unico; I was beginning to perceive the rudiments of a plan.

Sunday was non-existent; Monday particularly dreary. I sensed, without needing to ask him, that Tisserand had had a lousy weekend; this didn't surprise me in the least. It was already 22 December.

The following evening we went to eat in a pizzeria. The waiter had the air of actually being Italian; one imagined him to be both hairy and charming; he deeply disgusted me. On top of that he hurriedly set down our respective spaghettis without due care. Ah, if we'd been wearing slit skirts that would have been different!

Tisserand was knocking back huge glasses of wine; I was evoking different tendencies within contemporary dance music. He wasn't responding; in fact I don't think he was even listening. Nevertheless, when I briefly described the time-honoured alternation of fast and slow records, so as to underline the ritual character it had lent to the procedures of seduction, his interest was re-awakened (had he already had occasion, personally, to dance to a slow number? It was by no means certain). I went on to the offensive:

'I suppose you're doing something for Christmas. With the folks, no doubt . . .'

'We do nothing at Christmas, I'm Jewish,' he informed me with a touch of pride. 'At least, my parents are Jewish,' he added in an undertone.

This revelation shut me up for a few seconds. But after all, Jewish or not, did that really change anything? If so, I couldn't see what. I pressed on.

'What about doing something on the 24th? I know a club in Les Sables, *The Port of Call*. Very friendly . . .'

I had the feeling my words were ringing false; I was ashamed of myself. But Tisserand was no longer in any state to pay attention to such subtleties. 'Do you think there'll be lots of people? I get the impression the 24th is very "family",' that was his feeble, pathetic objection. I conceded that of course the 31st would be much better: 'Girls really like *to sleep around* on the 31st,' I asserted with authority. But for all that the 24th wasn't to be dismissed: 'Girls eat oysters with the parents and the grand-mother, receive their presents. But after midnight they go club-bing.' I was getting excited, believing my own story; Tisserand proved easy to convince, just as I'd predicted.

The following evening he took three hours to get ready. I waited for him while playing dominoes in the hotel lounge; I played both hands at once, it was really boring; all the same I was rather anxious.

He showed up dressed in a black suit and a gold tie; his hair must have taken him a good while; they make gels now that give the most surprising results. In the end a black outfit was what suited him best; poor schmuck.

We still had almost an hour to kill; there was no point in going clubbing before eleven-thirty, I was categorical about that. After a brief discussion we went to have a look-see at the midnight mass; the priest was speaking of an immense hope rising in the hearts of men; I found nothing to object to in that. Tisserand was getting bored, was thinking of other things; I began to feel somewhat disgusted, but I had to go through with it. I'd placed the steak knife in a plastic bag in the front of the car.

I found *The Port of Call* again without difficulty; I'd passed many a dull evening there, it has to be said. This was going back more than ten years; but unpleasant memories are erased less quickly than one thinks.

The club was half-full: mainly of twenty-five-year-olds, which immediately did for the modest chances of Tisserand. A lot of miniskirts, low-cut bustiers; in short, fresh meat. I saw his eyes suddenly pop out on taking in the dance floor; I left to order a bourbon at the bar. On my return he was already standing nervously at the edge of the clutch of dancers. I vaguely murmured 'Back in a minute', and made off towards a table whose slightly prominent position would afford me an excellent view of the theatre of operations.

To begin with Tisserand appeared to be interested in a twenty-something brunette, a secretary most like. I was highly inclined to approve of his choice. On the one hand the girl was no great beauty, and would doubtless be a pushover; her breasts, though good-sized, were already a bit slack, and her buttocks appeared flaccid; in a few years, one felt, all this would sag completely. On the other hand her somewhat audacious get-up unambiguously underlined her intention to find a sexual partner: her thin taffeta dress twirled with every movement, revealing a suspender belt and minuscule g-string in black lace which left her buttocks completely naked. To be sure, her serious, even slightly obstinate face seemed to indicate a prudent character; here was a girl who must surely carry condoms in her bag.

For a few minutes Tisserand danced not far from her, thrusting his arms forward energetically to indicate the enthusiasm the music caused in him. On two or three occasions he even clapped his hands to the beat; but the girl didn't seem to notice him in the least. Profiting from a short break between records he took the initiative and addressed a few words to her. She turned, threw him a scornful glance and took off across the dance floor to get away from him. That was that.

Everything was going as planned. I left to order a second bourbon at the bar.

On my return I sensed that something new was in the offing. A girl was sitting at the table next to mine, alone. She was much younger than Véronique, she might have been seventeen; that aside, she horribly resembled her. Her extremely simple, rather roomy beige dress did not really show off the contours of her body; they scarcely had need of it. The wide hips, the firm and smooth buttocks; the suppleness of the waist which leads the hands up to a pair of round, ample and soft breasts; the hands which rest confidently on the waist, espousing the noble rotundity of the hips. I knew it all; all I had to do was close my eyes to remember. Up to the face, full and candid, expressing the calm seduction of the natural woman, confident of her beauty. The calm serenity of the young filly, still frisky, eager to try out her limbs in a short gallop. The calm tranquillity of Eve, in love with her own nakedness, knowing herself to be obviously and eternally desirable. I realised that two years of separation had changed nothing; I knocked back my bourbon in one. This was the moment Tisserand chose to return; he was perspiring slightly; he spoke to me; I think he wished to know if I intended trying something with the girl. I didn't reply; I was starting to feel like vomiting, and I had a hard-on; things were at a pretty pass. I said 'Excuse me a moment,' and crossed the discothèque in the direction of the toilets. Once inside I put two fingers down my throat, but the amount of vomit proved feeble and disappointing. Then I masturbated with altogether greater success: I began thinking of Véronique a bit, of course, but then I concentrated on vaginas in general and that did the trick. Ejaculation came after a couple of minutes; it brought me a feeling of confidence and certainty.

On my return I saw that Tisserand had engaged in

conversation with the pseudo-Véronique; she was regarding him calmly and without contempt. I knew deep down that this young girl was a marvel; but it was no big deal, I'd done my masturbating. From the amorous point of view Véronique belonged, as we all do, to a *sacrificed generation*. She had certainly been capable of love; she would have wished to still be capable of it, I'll say that for her; but it was no longer possible. A scarce, artificial and belated phenomenon, love can only blossom under certain mental conditions, rarely conjoined, and totally opposed to the freedom of morals which characterises the modern era. Véronique had known too many discothèques, too many lovers; such a way of life impoverishes a human being, inflicting sometimes serious and always irreversible damage. Love as a kind of innocence and as a capacity for illusion, as an aptitude for epitomising the whole of the other sex in a single loved being rarely resists a year of sexual immorality, and never two. In reality the successive sexual experiences accumulated during adolescence undermine and rapidly destroy all possibility of projection of an emotional and romantic sort; progressively, and in fact extremely quickly, one becomes as capable of love as an old slag. And so one leads, obviously, a slag's life; in ageing one becomes less seductive, and on that account bitter. One is jealous of the young, and so one hates them. Condemned to remain unavowable, this hatred festers and becomes increasingly fervent; then it dies down and fades away, just as everything fades away. All that remains is resentment and disgust, sickness and the anticipation of death.

At the bar I managed to negotiate a bottle of bourbon with the barman for seven hundred francs. On turning round I banged into a young six-foot-six electrician. 'Hey, what's your problem?' he said in a not unfriendly tone; gazing up at him, I replied 'The milk of human kindness.' I saw my face in the mirror; it was gripped by a clearly unpleasant rictus. The electrician shook his head in resignation; I negotiated the crossing of the dance floor, bottle in hand; just before arriving at my destination I bumped into a woman at the cash desk and fell to the floor. Nobody helped me up. I was seeing the dancers' legs pumping all around me; I wanted to chop them off with an axe. The lighting effects were of an unbearable violence; I was in hell.

A group of boys and girls were sitting at our table; probably the pseudo-Véronique's classmates. Tisserand wasn't giving in, although he was starting to be a bit out of it; he was letting himself be progressively edged out of the conversation, as was all too obvious; and when one of the boys proposed buying a round at the bar he was already implicitly excluded. He nevertheless made the vague gesture of getting up, he tried to catch pseudo-Véronique's eye; in vain. Thinking better of it, he let himself fall back heavily on the banquette; completely huddled in on himself, he wasn't even aware of my presence; I poured myself another drink.

Tisserand's immobility was maintained for a minute or so; then he gave a sudden start, doubtless imputable to what is usually called 'the energy of despair'. Rising abruptly, he brushed past me as he made for the dance floor; his face was smiling and determined; he was still as ugly as ever, though.

Without hesitation he planted himself in front of a blonde and very sexy girl of about fifteen. She was wearing a short and skimpy dress of an immaculate white; perspiration had glued it to her body, and it was visible that she had nothing on underneath; her little round buttocks were moulded with perfect precision; one could clearly make out, stiffened by excitement, the brown aureolae of her breasts; the DJ had just announced fifteen minutes of oldies.

Tisserand invited her to jive; taken rather unawares, she accepted. From the very first chords of *Come On Everybody* I sensed he was about to screw up. He was swinging the girl around brutally, teeth clenched, a vicious look to him; each time he pulled her towards him he took the opportunity to plant his hand on her buttocks. As soon as the last notes played the young girl rushed off towards a group of girls her own age. Tisserand remained resolutely in the middle of the floor; he was slobbering slightly. The girl was pointing to him while speaking to her chums; she guffawed as she looked his way.

At this moment the pseudo-Véronique returned from the bar with her group of friends; she was deep in conversation with a young black guy, or rather half black. He was slightly older than her; I reckoned he could be about twenty. They came and sat down near our table; as they passed I gave a friendly little wave of the hand to the pseudo-Véronique. She looked at me in surprise but didn't react.

After the second rock number the DJ put on a slowie. It was Nino Ferrer's *Le Sud*; a magnificent record, it has to be said. The half-caste touched the pseudo-Véronique's shoulder lightly; they got up of common accord. At this instant Tisserand turned to face him. He spread his hands, opened his mouth, but I don't think he can have had time to speak. The half-caste eased him aside calmly, with gentleness, and in a few seconds they were on the dance floor.

They made a magnificent couple. The pseudo-Véronique was quite tall, maybe five seven, but he was a good head taller. She confidently pressed her body against the guy's. Tisserand sat down again at my side; he was trembling in every limb. He watched the couple, hypnotised. I waited a minute or more; this slowie, I recalled, went on for ever. Then I shook him gently by the shoulder, repeating 'Raphaël' over and again.

'What can I do?' he asked.

'Go and have a wank.'

'You reckon it's hopeless?'

'Sure. It's been hopeless for a long time, from the very beginning. Raphaël, you will never represent a young girl's erotic dream. You have to resign yourself to the inevitable; such things are not for you. It's already too late, in any case. The sexual failure you've known since your adolescence, Raphaël, the frustration that has followed you since the age of thirteen, will leave their indelible mark. Even supposing that you might have women in the future – which in all frankness I doubt – this will not be enough; nothing will ever be enough. You will always be an orphan to those adolescent loves you never knew. In you the wound is already deep; it will get deeper and deeper. An atrocious, unremitting bitterness will end up gripping your heart. For you there will be neither redemption nor deliverance. That's how it is. Yet that doesn't mean, however, that all possibility of revenge is closed to you. These women you desire so much, you too can possess them. You can even possess what is most precious about them. What is it, Raphaël, that is most precious about them?'

'Their beauty?' he suggested.

'It's not their beauty, I can tell you that much; it isn't their vagina either, nor even their love; because all these disappear with life itself. And from now on you can possess their life. Launch yourself on a career of murder this very evening; believe me, my friend, it's the only way still open to you. When you feel these women trembling at the end of your knife, and begging for their young lives, then will you truly be the master; then will you possess them body and soul. Perhaps you will even manage, prior to their sacrifice, to obtain various succulent favours from them; a knife, Raphaël, is a powerful ally.'

He was staring long and hard at the couple who were intertwined as they slowly turned around the dance floor; one of the pseudo-Véronique's hands encircled the half-caste's waist, the other was resting on his shoulder. Softly, almost timidly, he said to me, 'I'd rather kill the guy.' I knew then that I'd won; I suddenly relaxed and refilled our glasses.

'Well then,' I exclaimed, 'what's stopping you? Why yes! Get the hang of it on a young nigger! In any case they're going to leave together, the thing looks cut and dried. You'll have, of course, to kill the guy before getting a piece of the woman. As it happens I've a knife in the front of the car.'

They did in fact leave together ten minutes later. I got up, grabbing the bottle as I did so; Tisserand followed me docilely.

Outside, the night was oddly pleasant, warm almost. There was a brief confab in the parking lot between the girl and the black guy; they made off towards a moped. I got into the front of the car, took the knife out of its bag; its serrations gleamed prettily in the moonlight. Before getting on the moped they embraced for some time; it was beautiful and very tender. By my side Tisserand was trembling incessantly; I had the feeling I could smell the putrid sperm rising in his prick. Playing nervously with the controls, he dipped the headlights; the girl blinked. They decided then to leave; our car moved off gently behind them. Tisserand asked me:

'Where are they going to sleep?'

'Probably at the girl's parents; it's the done thing. But we'll have to stop them before then. As soon as we're on a back road we'll run into the moped. They'll probably be a bit banged up; you won't have any problem finishing off the guy.'

The car was bowling smoothly along the coast road; ahead, in the beam of the headlights, the girl could be seen clutching the waist of her companion. After a few minutes' silence I started in again:

'We could always drive over them, just to be on the safe side.'

'They don't look to be concerned about anything,' he remarked in a dreamy voice.

Suddenly the moped veered off to the right along a track going down to the sea. This wasn't in the plan; I told Tisserand to slow down. A bit further on the couple pulled up; I noticed that the guy was taking the trouble to set his anti-theft device before leading the girl off towards the dunes.

Once over the first lot of dunes I understood more. Almost at high tide, and forming an immense curve, the sea extended to our feet; the light of the full moon was playing gently on its surface. The couple were making off towards the south, skirting the edge of the water. The air temperature was increasingly pleasant, abnormally pleasant; you'd have thought it was June. In these conditions, well, sure, I understood: to make love beside the ocean, under the splendour of the stars; I understood only too well; it's exactly what I'd have done in their place. I proffered the knife to Tisserand; he left without a word.

I went back towards the car; supporting myself on the bonnet, I slid down on to the sand. I gulped down a few mouthfuls of bourbon, then got behind the wheel and steered the car in the direction of the sea. It was a bit risky, but the sound of the engine itself seemed muffled, imperceptible; the night was all-embracing, tender. I had a terrible yearning to drive straight into the ocean. Tisserand's absence was becoming prolonged.

When he returned he didn't say a word. He was holding the long knife in his hand; the blade was glinting softly; I detected no bloodstains on its surface. All of a sudden I felt a wave of sadness. Finally, he spoke.

'When I got there they were lying between two dunes. He'd already taken her dress and her bra off. Her breasts were so beautiful, so round in the moonlight. Then she turned, she lay on top of him. She unbuttoned his trousers. When she began sucking him off I couldn't stand it.'

He fell silent. I waited. The sea was as smooth as a lake.

'I turned back, I walked between the dunes. I could have killed them; they were oblivious to everything, they didn't even know I was there. I masturbated. I had no wish to kill them; blood changes nothing.'

'Blood is everywhere.'

'I know. Sperm is everywhere too. Right now I've had enough. I'm going back to Paris.'

He didn't suggest that I accompany him. I got up, walked towards the sea. The bottle of bourbon was almost empty; I swallowed the last mouthful. When I got back the beach was deserted; I hadn't even heard the car drive off.

I was never to see Tisserand again; he was killed in his car that night, on his return trip to Paris. There was a lot of fog on the outskirts of Angers; he was driving like the clappers, as usual. His 205 GTI collided head-on with a lorry that had pulled out into the middle of the carriageway. He died instantly, just before dawn. The next day was a holiday, to celebrate the birth of Christ; it was only three days later that his family heard about the business. The burial had already taken place, according to ritual; which cut short any idea of wreaths or mourners. A few words were pronounced on the sadness of such a death and on the difficulty of driving in fog, people went back to work, and that was that.

At least, I said to myself on learning of his death, he'll have battled to the end. The Under-25s club, the winter sports vacations . . . At least he won't have abdicated, won't have thrown in the towel. Right to the end, and despite repeated failure, he'll have looked for love. Squashed flat in the bodywork of his 205 GTI on the almost deserted highway, all bloody in his black suit and gold tie, I know that in his heart there was still the struggle, the desire and the will to struggle.

Guillaume Dustan

Serge the Beauty & Rendezvous

Guillaume Dustan

We met him at the Queen fairly late, at an hour when there's practically nobody left but fanatic clubbers. Going bald. Six-one, one hundred and seventy-five pounds. Body a knockout. White even-spaced teeth in a perpetual smile. Sufficiently young. Nice face. Visibly blitzed on some high-quality stuff. First we looked at each other. Then I was dancing, clinging to Stéphane, to turn him on. He moved in. We were putting on a show on the dance floor, making like we were humping one another. This got a rise out of him. I felt quantity there. Then we got unglued and exchanged a few words through the din of the music. I sent Stéphane to get us something to drink. To the other one I said Man do I ever want to blow you. He said No problem. He led me off to the toilets. I said to myself Cool, he knows what he wants. I followed with no resistance. There was a traffic jam at the toilets, a whole line to get in. I said All right what do we do? He dragged me over to a blind spot just by the doorway.

He turned his back to the dance floor. I let myself slide to my knees. He brought out his mega-beautiful dick and I took it in my face and jerked off for five minutes or so. This was hot. Then I said Look my boyfriend is waiting for us, we gotta go over to him, OK? He said OK. Stéphane was waiting at the bar with the drinks, very cool as always.

We rather rapidly agreed as to the next steps. First, we stop by his place to do a new American drug I haven't heard of that's supposed to be great for fucking, and after we go home because we have toys at our place and he doesn't at his. By now I'm fairly convinced that this is going to be more trouble than it's worth because of this final detail, but he is such a specimen I cannot imagine one single second not getting him when I can.

His apartment is tiptop. Loft space. TV and speakers in the bathroom. Classy furniture. An envelope addressed to him from a TV network is lying on the extra-large counter of his eat-in American kitchen. He puts on Trance very loud. The sound is the best. We taste his powder. In ten minutes we are wiped out. Lights camera action. Our clothes peel off. He is sublime. Great dick, very large and long, big balls with lots of skin. I suck him. I lick his balls. He smacks my back, my ass. He plays macho man. I like. He's like, You're a real slut, a true one. You get me all hot and bothered. I check. He exaggerates. I'm sure he's not going to bang me but too bad. In the bathroom there was an old box of Prophyltex, full, and Prophyltex is much too tight for a cock like his. If he was using condoms inside an ass with any frequency he'd have Manix large. What's weird also is a pair of very classy women's high heels on the floor by the mirror in his bedroom. But it's the only trace of woman in the whole space. Maybe he's bi, the pretentious prick. He looks me in the eye. I do the same. We smile. He tells me Don't you look at me like that if you don't want me marrying you. I tell him It's not my fault, that's the way it is. He's like, wow wow wow!, clapping his hands while I paddle his ass with my hands to make for a sexier ambience. And then the darling is too stoned, and falls asleep on the parquet with his leather pants down to his ankles. I like this Serge, that's for sure, it's like being in love. The problem is, of course, he's not fucking me. Just a bump or two of the cock, no condom, like that, in the kitchen, the windows open, after he's snapped his cordless telephone antenna trying to insert it up my ass. This guy is not used to fucking, it shows. True you can't have everything in life. He tells me several times how sorry he is he's so wasted. I tell him no big deal.

He falls asleep on the sofa while I'm sucking him. The stereo plays opera now, this must be what he usually listens to. I'm left alone. I go into his bedroom, I scope out a few books, a method for a perfect body and how to train it, under the table by the bed, the cassettes under the TV in front of the bed, no porn or else they're well hidden, a dresser with jockey shorts, boxer shorts, socks, handkerchiefs. I try on a pair of blue jockey shorts, not bad, then a jockstrap, not nice (I used to have the same one almost), then an old pair of Nikos, ultra-hot cut that look great on me. I put them in my jacket, then I search for a container for the powder. I find an empty film container on his desk. I extract my little present. I wolf down a slice of all-bran bread. There's nothing else in the fridge. The opera's still on. I wake Stéphane. You all right? He's OK. I leave Serge the beauty a note with our telephone number. It's nice outside. I put on my shades. The streets are already coming to life. We go home. Stéphane drives. Parking lot. Pains au chocolat. Croissants. The baker's son is still our fan. It's good to be home. So we smoke a joint. And I fuck Stéphane.

He calls around seven, eight in the evening. Hi, it's Sergio. That's what I called him in my note. He's going to dinner, but we can meet up later. He is weird. He says I'll call back at midnight. All right, this is normal, with three it's always a little complicated. But for once there's someone who interests me. Makes an impression, the Fuck. I'm sure he's not even going to call me back.

He calls back, only it's one-thirty. This looks bad. He apologises. I cut him short. His dinner's not over, can we meet at the Folies at three, no better make it three-thirty? I say OK. I hang up. I tell Stéphane Look, I want this fuck so bad just this once for real. I've got to go. Stéphane says it's not a problem.

I'm at the Folies Pigalle. There's a very beautiful girl in a hot pink ultra-tight T-shirt, with Babie written in silver. She dances great. She's as flashy as a faggot or a black. It's three o'clock. I did a quarter hit of acid, three lines of coke, smoked two joints and drank a beer at home before going out. High, but not too high. I chat with a cab driver. On the door of the Folies there's a guy Quentin and I had a threesome with ages ago. He says hi to me. Are you with somebody? A wave of paranoia, I don't understand what he wants to say, I tell him no I'm by myself, can I come in? He looks at me a little surprised but he's got to see I'm stoned. Once I'm in I tell myself obviously he's not going to turn away somebody he knows. And I think Wow, it's cool, I know the doorman at the Folies. This sort of stuff impresses me. I know it's stupid. Then there's a Chinese guy at the entrance, one of the organisers, he's real real tall and thin, he makes come-fuck-me T-shirts as a sideline. I ran into him at a fashion show my friend Georges took me to. He bends over nearly in two and gives me this lifeless kiss. Hi! I buy myself a beer. I smoke. I dance.

Tonight I know absolutely not a soul in here. No buddy, no pick-up, nobody I've ever exchanged more than two words with before. This stresses me a little. Plus, the acid's strong. It gives me these pains in the back and it pulls on the cheekbones and I'm speeding, zooming, and from time to time I'm a little short of breath and I have hot rushes. I calm down, tell myself it's always like this on acid. There are the positive sides too, the light and the colours are ten times more real than in reality. Since I'm having a good trip I can't think about anything disagreeable for more than two seconds. My one and only preoccupation has to do with what I'm feeling and this absolute necessity of mine to move, to discharge the really excessive energy the acid gives me.

Only three o'clock. I decided to be here at two-thirty to be sure not to miss him. I get off on playing the ditz. The music is good, the sound is better than before and makes me dance. When I take acid dancing relaxes my back. First I warm up, and then when I'm really cooking I get up on the stage, I take off my T-shirt, I dance with no shirt, my braces trailing down my thighs on top of my combat boots. It's best to have on big shoes when you have a tendency to fall around.

And then the music turns not as good, too hardcore. I come off the stage. I'm dripping sweat. I go to the toilet to freshen up. Long pink corridor. There are some North African girls getting a rise out of some North African guys. One girl's saying she can piss like a guy, in the urinal. I wasn't able to piss anyhow, so I move away for her to show us. She comes up, unzips, and then she chickens out. They jabber a little aggressively, that's North Africa cruising. I go to empty my bladder in a closed stall that opens just then. The ambience is bizarre tonight.

The evening is a mega-success I think. There are only beautiful people who dance so well everybody looks filled with wonder, totally trashed or else very new to the club scene, or even both. Nothing to cruise. Too trendy. Whatever. Acid makes it OK.

I don't care so much for acid, I think it's too strong, but all right, let's face it, acid does give you zip. As soon as the music is a little less hardcore Trance, I go back and dance all the way down. Hard-hitting DJ chains together deep disco shake-that-ass, Trance pumped up to where it is almost too much reality, the dance floor begins to lay down its arms when UP! it begins all over again. Guys cry out in pain when the DJ breaks the rhythm on purpose in the middle of a mix. I take a break. Stairways.

Gallery. Bar. I'm covered in sweat, looking a little too hardcore for a place like this, I'm not served right away, but in the end it's OK, the gin and peppermint is good.

Ten to four and he's a no-show. I go out alone. I walk around Place Pigalle. I'm in a rage. When I get to the Transfert the doorman smiles at me. Stéphane is there, with his big gentle eyes, a slutty tank top plunging to his tits. A kiss of the tongue and then I say What's up, cutie? He says Nothing, I was getting a little bored. The fucking fuck bar. The anniversary of the Transfert. Nothing is worse than a festive occasion in an S & M venue. Cake is being passed around on paper plates. Nobody wants any, but to be polite the guys closest to the bar force themselves. The bartender has his little tantrum: No cake gentlemen? Well let me remind you there are plenty of people out there who would.

I go around the back of the backroom, suck a little the skinhead boy hanging out naked in the big sink everybody uses for pissing. What he wants in fact is my piss, but I don't want to piss. I split. I get a few kisses, two guys tweak my nipples. I do the same to them. The guy in front of me sticks two fingers up my ass. I pull up my pants. I turn around. There's a guy in front of me I know but haven't got around to yet. He goes out all the time but I don't think he does a lot of fucking. He looks at my cock. I stroke it a little in front of him for fun. I have a discussion with a little skinhead who looks like a mouse. He's extra sweet. I tell him You make me want to do bad things. He's like, I do?, full of hope. But I'm not that convinced, I don't think he's slutty enough. He senses this as well, and we let things go at that. I go back to Stéphane at the bar. We get champagne squirted all over our faces. This is beginning to weigh down on me. We decide to leave.

In the car I'm wiped. Stéphane tells me five or six times he wants sex. I don't answer. When we peel off our clothing at home, the carpet around the bed gets covered with confetti. I say to Stéphane If you want to get fucked I can do it. He doesn't look like he believes. I ask Is your ass clean? He says Yes. I take out an Olla, we don't have any Manix large, but I really like Olla. They're the ones we used in the Quentin days. They are kind of thick, but very supple and soft. I bang him first standing in front of the toilet. I make him put his head in and I fuck him. Then I bring him back to the bedroom and I fuck him on the bed, from the front, then from behind. It lasts a long time, and it's really not bad, I enter and I exit, his ass is like slurp, slurp slurp, very loud, he groans and moans, bunched up under me. I begin to lose my hard-on, his ass is too wide. I continue though. And then we have to stop because I've gone too soft. We go wash our hands. I propose he fuck me. He says he wants to piss. I flop into the tub and he pisses on me and I don't wash it off and we return to the bed. The fucking is great. Deep. Long. I let myself get fucked like never before. I find he's getting better and better. And then it becomes obvious we're too stoned to come. I search around for my watch. It's ten o'clock, we've been fucking four hours. We finish off the easy way, he licks my balls, I come, and then I offer to work over his ass with my left hand because my right hand's got cum all over it. He explodes. We cuddle. I roll one last joint. He falls asleep. I smoke half and then I realise I'm losing consciousness so I put the joint down and fall asleep.

I awake livid because of the no-show last night. We watch TV. I try to resist and then give in and call Serge around seven in the evening. Machine. I speak in case he's screening. He picks up.

'Yes?'

'Hi, it's Guillaume.'

'Hi, you all right?'

'No.'

'Ahh . . . I have people over right now, my mother.'

'That's nice.'

'How was it last night?'

I think this over.

'It was disappointing. I mean I didn't know you weren't going to come.'

'Me neither. I didn't know I wasn't going to come.'

Silence.

'Well,' I go on, 'you're with people and anyway I don't have a whole lot else to tell you. It's up to you.'

'I'll call you back.'

'OK.'

I hang up. This guy makes me sick. Do you realise he

stands me up and I call him back, I say to Stéphane? But this is what's good about it too. Being impressed. Showing it. Like a slut. But not too much. I was happy that it had been disappointing. I was hoping he'd understand I meant to say both that he was a disappointment and that I was disappointed. I wanted to rattle his cage a little. But at the same time I still wanted him. His ultra-soft skin. His perfect muscles, not too big, not too small. Beautiful.

Agnès Desarthe

Transient Bliss

'**O**h go on, put some make-up on,' said Viviane, emerging from the shower. 'I said I'd lend you mine. I've got everything you need. And you're dark, like me, we've got the same colouring.'

'I'd rather not,' replied Cyrille.

'But I've never seen you with make-up. I bet you look absolutely *brill*. I'll help you if you like. I'll be the beautician. You sit there and I'll do your face. I'll keep it very light. I'm ever so sensitive to my client's personality,' added Viviane giving Cyrille a handbag mirror.

Cyrille let Viviane have her way. She closed her eyelids, opened her mouth, looked up at the ceiling, blotted her red lacquered lips with a Kleenex, turned to the right, then to the left, and even allowed her colleague to run a comb through her short, tangled hair.

'There we are, Madam. I hope Madam is pleased. Anyway, the first session's free.'

Cyrille held out the mirror which she had placed in her lap at the beginning of the operation and looked at herself, swallowing with difficulty. She looked forty-five.

'Do you like it? You've got gorgeous eyes, you know. At first, I was a bit embarrassed by your, what's it called, I don't mean you're cross-eyed . . .'

'My divergent strabismus?'

'Yes, that's it. At first it's sort of weird, but actually, once you get used to it, it's rather attractive. It's kind of original.

Do you see the way I've done your eyeliner? I can never do it like that on me.'

'I need to get used to it. Don't you think it makes me look old?'

'No way. It gives you a bit of . . . pzazz. It does, honestly. It's amazing. Hang on, I haven't finished,' added Viviane going over to the wardrobe. 'I've just remembered a little . . . hold on while I look for it . . . here!' she cried, yanking a ball of midnight blue fabric down from a shelf. Look at this little basque. Isn't it *great?*'

Cyrille smiled, unable to part her lips, gummed together by the lipstick.

'It's a bit tight on me,' said Viviane, 'but it's gor-geous. It'll fit you like a glove. Go on, try it on.'

Might as well, thought Cyrille, going into the bathroom to get changed.

'You see, I told you!' exclaimed Viviane as her colleague came out wearing the basque, her shoulders hunched and her arms riveted to her sides. 'Go on, walk around, let's see how it looks when you move. Don't just stand there. You look like a little kid.'

'What do you want me to do?' asked Cyrille.

'I don't know, lift your arms up. Remember we'll be dancing this evening.'

Cyrille did as she was told. She raised her arms and gyrated.

'Faster, faster,' urged Viviane. 'What the hell are you doing? You look like a stuffed dummy.'

Cyrille began again, putting a bit more life into it, and Viviane began to clap her hands and sing *Be-bop-a-lula*. I feel a complete idiot, thought Cyrille, wiggling her hips. But before she could think of an answer, a sudden jerk made the elastic holding up the basque slip, revealing her breasts.

Her hands flew up to cover them, and she felt herself blush.

'It doesn't matter,' said Viviane, trying to take her arm, 'no one can see you.'

Cyrille dodged her and rushed into the bathroom, locking the door.

'I don't know what got into you,' said Viviane as they surfaced from the Métro. 'It looked great on you. What did you wash your face with? Now it's all blotchy. And just look at your eyes. Why the hell are you still crying, we're there. Look, you see the café over there?'

Cyrille nodded.

'And those two guys in the window, can you see them? Well, I warn you, they're our charming escorts for the evening, so stop that, will you, before you do any more damage.'

Cyrille sniffed, balled her fists against her eyelids and smiled at Viviane.

'I'm sorry,' she said. 'I don't know what came over me. I'm not used to all this.'

Viviane patted her shoulder and dragged her on.

'Don't worry about it. We're not going to let it spoil the evening, are we?'

Cyrille shook her head and allowed herself to be piloted across the road.

Cyrille looked at Jean-Marc who didn't take his eyes off Michel, clinging to him for support. He had tired blond hair and an attractive triangular face with slightly effeminate features. His hands were particularly delicate and agile, and Cyrille told herself it could have been worse. He offered her a cigarette. She took it. Viviane frowned, then relaxed. Cyrille batted her eyelids, pleading with her not to say anything. From the first puff, she felt sick and giddy. She gripped the banquette with one hand and looked up at the ceiling. The mouldings started to swim. Cyrille felt as though she was falling. She took another drag and a cloud of smoke made her eyes smart. She closed her eyelids to keep back her tears. The giddiness grew worse, melting her body and making her deaf and blurring her vision.

Jean-Marc and Michel were talking about a band, a jazz band. Viviane nodded enthusiastically. The orange juice mixed with the taste of tobacco was foul. Cyrille felt like a laboratory mouse being tested for a new drug. She tried to keep as still as possible. The only sounds coming from her were stomach rumbles. Say something, she thought. She raised her hand to call the waiter, and paid the bill.

'It's my round,' she announced, groggily.

The two men smiled at her. She'd have done better to keep quiet.

Michel was at the wheel. Viviane sat in front with him. Cyrille and Jean-Marc were in the back, like children, clinging to the seat to avoid accidentally touching each other should the car round a bend too sharply. They didn't look at each other, didn't exchange a word. As fun guys go, he's a dead loss, thought Cyrille, as if it mattered, as if she were disappointed by her escort's shyness. He could have been one-eyed, obese, had a stutter, or even all three. What the hell did it matter? Her life wasn't at stake. To convince herself, she only had to repeat the unutterably spiritual adage Viviane had made up that afternoon: 'Going to a club means going to a club, that's all.'

On her way down to the basement, Cyrille missed a stair and fell headlong against Jean-Marc. At the same time, as he caught her by the arm and asked if she had hurt herself, a door slammed at the foot of the stairs, releasing a smell of urine and rose-scented air freshener. Rubbing her ankle, Cyrille wrinkled up her nose and wished she'd broken her leg. The thought of an ambulance whisking her far away from there, on a stretcher covered by a white sheet with ironed-in creases, seemed like the only escape.

'Not a drop of alcohol and drunk already,' cracked Michel.

Cyrille clenched her teeth and saw from Viviane's lover's smile that he was joking, the way fifteen-year-olds do, to cover up the fact that they're embarrassed and prefer to hurt others rather than look foolish. It was her turn to smile. She ran her hands through her hair and opened her eyes exaggeratedly wide.

'Do you come here often?' she asked Jean-Marc.

He nodded.

'Mates of ours are playing this evening,' he added.

Cyrille raised her eyebrows enquiringly, to show that she was interested, but Jean-Marc didn't say another word. He found her a seat and went off to go and say hello to his friends.

Her legs crossed, her head throbbing with the music and her eyes already prickling from the cigarette smoke, she watched Jean-Marc and Michel moving among the low tables, smacking the palms of other guys, who looked just like them, in ritual greeting. She wondered if they all had secret names, like boy scouts.

Viviane was at the bar, one buttock precariously balanced on a stool that was too high, one shoulder bare, her head nodding in time to the music. She was a different Viviane from the one Cyrille knew, and Cyrille had the impression that this was the true Viviane: sensual, nonchalant, tossing back her hair to show off her face when someone succeeded in making her laugh.

On the stage, five musicians, some standing, others sitting, but all wearing hats, were playing, their eyes closed. They opened them only to glance to left or right, to check the tonality, the tempo at the beginning or end of a solo, agreeing to come in on the coda; or at least that's what Cyrille imagined, plonking her knowledge of chamber music onto these pieces that she couldn't make head or tail of and that made her feel old. The double-bass player wearing a multicoloured embroidered cap smiled, a cigarette wedged between his teeth. The smoke rose blue towards the ceiling, splitting his face in two. Cyrille wondered how he managed not to choke. She decided to keep her eyes on him. At least she would feel she was doing something, understanding. But why not let herself go too? Tap her foot gently, or get up casually and start dancing on the spot? That's what the others around her were doing. They weren't worrying about anything, were they? They weren't wondering how the double bass player managed not to choke. Look at him, she told herself. Look at him, and switch off.

A woman with spangled tights and a velvet frock-coat trod on her foot and spilled Cyrille's drink in her lap as she leaned over to apologise. Cyrille felt like bursting into tears and quickly turned away her head. She was too hot and went to find Jean-Marc to tell him she wanted to leave. Before her rose a wall of bodies swaying over islands formed by motionless feet. Her gaze was drawn to a glass that someone sitting two tables away seemed to be holding out to her. She stood up, thinking that she was being taken quite simply for a tart.

He was an elderly man, clearly delighted to be there, slightly slumped in his seat, a champagne bucket in front of him. He was drinking whisky. Cyrille asked him, as she sat down beside him and accepted the glass he was proffering, if he didn't like champagne.

'I drink Scotch,' he replied, 'like in the movies.'

He had a foreign accent. His small hairless chin and the mop of white locks over his forehead gave him an effeminate air.

'I can't dance,' Cyrille told him, 'I feel so out of place.'

'Drink,' he urged her.

Cyrille obeyed. She waited for him to place his hand on her thigh, but he didn't budge, continuing to take little sips, his eyes laughing, his hands trembling slightly.

'Do you come here often?' Cyrille asked him, with such a strong feeling of déjà vu that she thought she must be mad.

The old man clicked his tongue and shook his head.

'No,' he said in a drawl. 'I never come here. It's my grand-son who told me to. He plays jazz. I got it all wrong. I thought he was playing this evening.' He shrugged and added: 'I'm more into bop.'

Cyrille nodded, wishing that she could reply 'me too'.

The old man put down his glass with a sigh of satisfaction, licked his lips and refilled Cyrille's glass.

'What about you?' he asked. 'Do you come here often?'

'This is the first time. It's a . . . I mean it's a colleague, well, a friend from work who brought me. That girl over there, at the bar.'

'Little Viviane? Ah! Pretty girl, isn't she?'

Cyrille gawped at him.

'I said, pretty girl, Viviane,' he repeated, louder, thinking she hadn't heard. 'My grandson only brings back nincompoops. Maybe he's gay, how should I know?'

'I'm with him,' said Cyrille, suddenly struck by the resemblance between the old man and Jean-Marc.

The elderly man raised his glass in a toast.

'You are a pearl,' he said, 'a right little natural pearl.'

Cyrille smiled and slid down against the banquette.

She felt her eyes begin to sparkle.

'Come on,' said Jean-Marc, taking her hand. Cyrille saw him dart a furious look at his grandfather while she got to her feet and, as if to make up for the insult, held out her hand to the old man.

'I'm very pleased to have met you,' she said.

'Not half as pleased as me,' he replied.

'He's a right pain,' said Jean-Marc, slipping his arm around Cyrille's waist.

'What are you doing?' she asked. 'Do you want to dance?'

'No, yes, who cares? It's the only way you can get to talk. Anyway, nobody's looking at us.'

Cyrille knew that wasn't true. The old man was looking at them. She wound her arm around Jean-Marc's neck and pretended to dance with him, her head slightly cocked to one side to catch what he was saying.

'He's a pain, I tell you. Completely senile. I don't know what the hell he's doing here.'

'He thought you were playing this evening.'

Jean-Marc shook his head.

'I never said that.'

'So how did he get the address? He said he never came here.'

'I gave it to him, of course. He always wants to know everything. He acts as though I was still fourteen. I live with him, so he thinks he has a right. I've always got to tell him where I'm going.'

'He's interested in you, that's all.'

Cyrille felt foolish for saying that.

'Sorry,' she added, 'that's cheap psychology, it's rubbish. I don't know what's wrong with me. Normally . . . normally . . .'

'What?'

'Nothing.'

'Normally what? You say what?'

'Nothing, I don't know.'

'Go on, say it, say it.'

He hugged her close and Cyrille felt his breath on her cheek. She was surprised not to feel disgusted, and lingered for a moment, her face close to his, her eyes shut, breathing in the sweet, gentle fragrance of his mouth. She opened her eyes a fraction and looked at his tiny, white, inoffensive teeth, behind an irrepressible smile. Her arms began to tremble. She kissed

Jean-Marc, thinking of the old man who was watching them. And then her mind went blank.

It was he who broke away. They looked at each other, as innocent as children who amuse themselves pulling off insects' legs to while away the summer holidays. He left his hand in hers for a long time. Cyrille glanced in the direction of the old man and noticed he had disappeared. She thought of the Cheshire cat whose grin lives on and, feeling suddenly ashamed at having made such an exhibition of herself, hoped he had left before witnessing it.

'Your grandfather's not there any more,' she said.

Jean-Marc smiled at her without answering and made his way to the exit.

The men put their arms around each other's shoulders and the women walked arm in arm. Cyrille could feel Viviane clutching her especially tight. In the car, they didn't talk much. They smoked a lot.

'How about one last drink?' suggested Michel.

'No,' said Cyrille. 'I'm going home.'

She was glued to the right-hand door, and Jean-Marc to the left. As soon as they had felt the night air, they had resumed their defensive positions. Viviane turned to Cyrille with an enquiring pout. Cyrille frowned and Viviane shrugged, shaking her head a little too vigorously. A hairpin fell out of her topknot and landed on the back seat. Jean-Marc and Cyrille's hands collided as they groped for the little scrap of metal. They had both wanted to pick the thing up, but neither of them was prepared to do so if the price was prolonged contact. Simultaneously, they withdrew their fingers burned by shame and put them back where they belonged, in the warm, clenched in their closed fists. Cyrille thought that, in ten years' time, the car would be sold for scrap and the hairpin would be crushed with the rest.

Lorette Nobécourt

Irritation

Well, I was born paralysed. Semi-paralysed. Half so. Medicine neglected to turn me round correctly. Half-paralysed. So it won't come as a surprise that *they* would have wanted to get rid of me; at birth, I knew everything, I was going to see everything, say everything. It was simple: either *they* would kill me or I would speak. Struggle to the death. *They* drove me towards windows, rivers, roadways; *they* slapped me with ludicrous ailments like excrements of madness to live on my skin. Death or dementia!

Ever since the first day, the first hour, I have regularly wished to overthrow the world so as to straighten the workings of my arteries. I found myself in a thought in need of twisting; twisting thought to the North in order to lessen somewhat the *noisying* din of my dried-up vessels, up there, to the brain. The blood stayed in my nerves. I danced above, below.

I am the child who sees, who knows, the child-witness born at night in the drama of terrifying deformity, with blood that wouldn't flow, of the stiff leg, the worn brain, the broken arm. I was born in parental panic. Dearly paid.

After my birth, it took less than six months for a monumental psoriasis to appear, the proof of my infamy and my difference, scabies in other words, the sort that is treated with arsenic in small, regular injections; my skin condition, a palpable symptom for all eyes to see and eventually for mine as well. Through the years, the affliction would sporadically turn into a pale callous membrane that invaded my mouth, thus setting me apart, like the insane.

From now on, I am of all stories. I am God since it is all the same to me whether or not there is a God. I am everybody since I am nobody. Since I no longer have a role to play; since I have ceased to have the least idea of what I was to be, having thus finally become – neither angel nor beast, only graciously leaning above the abyss – this vertiginous equilibrium, exulting each day, with rage, to apprehend the infallible in joy.

Unfortunately, fear will never cease and kings will still have as many wars to indulge in as nations to tyrannise. Yes, but now joy holds me.

With an unconcealed delight, I bared the obscenity of my inner flesh. I dug into my skin, I was looking for the enigma, the moving knowledge, the suspected monster, the debauched intimate, under my perforated swellings, this live force like a belly waiting to be opened. To discover this flesh, yes, the unsayable which we never see, the dark side, hidden and black. The horror of this unruly brewing, I wanted it – that was what I pursued relentlessly. I turned myself inside out like a glove, a real-life myology that I improvised as I squandered myself. I would scalp myself, thus becoming useless, a bad machine, removed from the great industry ... And the gaping scarifications I left trailing on my skin tissues were so many proofs of my oddity and my difference. For I wilfully condemned myself to refusing that frugal good-health indispensable for professional life, necessary to the grotesque masquerade of social play-acting. Healthy: the others were so more by terror than by choice. I held on to my illness as a definition. No obligation for me to give explanations, my face itself displayed my refusal, it was good. They called me guilty and diabolical: for allowing myself to be invaded by my pityriasis. I knew I was lucid, on the way towards a pure interiority, close to indifference, towards an unbearable toxicity. I had nothing left to share with the outside. I was still a cause for worry, my body showed no resistance, no, I didn't hold back any of what was running wild. I let a thousand horses gallop, unbridled, under my rind ... waste all over my fabric, among my wounds ... I displayed my traces, I called myself alive, no amount of control could do anything against the splatters I nourished as an assurance of being conscious, at the very heart of that sharp pleasure: the gratification of the itching claiming its due. Yes, my itching, which I hated before adoring it, for only it knew how to tear me apart, blow my guts, light up my flesh like so many factories in the night, flickering across my skin. A miserly existence: that was what I would henceforth reject, I defined my enemy, I revelled in my obsession. To risk letting go of the insides, letting them spread outwards, and despite the moral oppression, to never cease mingling with this orgiastic state ... My body as a bad machine, yes, I was *economically dysfunctional*, and that flooded me with a drunkenness as yet unknown, left for me to explore, to live day by day. In so disembowelling myself, I didn't stop sinning in the eyes of the others and glorifying myself in my own. I *should* have taken care of myself, I *should* have taken some of that soporific, debilitating medicine, some of those vile shots which make you docile for the rest of the week. Calm down: they all wanted me to calm down, to take care of myself. To calm down, to take care of the excessive nervousness revealed by the outbursts . . . Nervous I was indeed, my nerves tensed like a bow crazed for that fatal arrow aimed at the cleaving of a new freedom. I liked that, to mess up this inside, to sow panic in my stunned limbs, suddenly naked, flayed by the cold air. I dug at the skin because it was the only way to refuse any attachment to a confused world that oozed debilitation. Fertile work: my proliferating unruliness, my luxurious decline. Such a vulgar, nobly vulgar, savagery in my epidermic frenzy, devised by me alone and no other, this itching which was the signature of a wholly personal creation, the auspicious reaction which I had inserted into my life at the very beginning of days, my master work, my absolute proof. I had come very close to surrendering to their awful industriousness. Now, it wasn't only the family that I rejected, no: but them, all the others, the happily servile ones, whereas my blood was me, and my body my unity: a massive block electrified by its tendons, its disarming volts, white demented wires which charged my joy. And my incredible muscles supporting my blackened flesh, my deep muscles, like a net tightening around my intimate truth. I forbade myself any form of tyranny, I gave in to the onerous exuberance of my ailment, I rejected any talk that smelled of the social and of the smug well-being. Their hygienic thoughts disgusted me.

In those crawling nights, I would interrogate the secret of my sheath. I would decipher the enigma, I wanted to understand what was hidden behind the inscrutable figure, the obscure black lie, the darkest and most archaic lie, that of servility. There is no law, no norm, no schema, they had all lied to me. Behind my epidermis, I was discovering the truth of an unsuspected world, I was conquering the power to choose, on a large scale, for oneself, and from then on I knew new pleasures. Like the serpent crawling on its bad skin, I left behind the exquisite lie of the false; I ran into my own bones which I haven't ceased gnawing at since. For however bare, I was still clothed, and however bare, the world still stank. I clawed at my skin as I clawed at that thick callus which readily covers beliefs. In an all too pinched laughter, I jostled against myself: they were a thousand and a hundred waiting to burst, those who tore my hide, who guided all my nails onto the rough surface of my taut thinking. I let myself go along with the exquisite orgy of this perverse rising. Rejected by my kind and by this purulent world, I gained access to an unknown freedom, one which the itching alone could grant me.

My skin was bursting like the world I had inherited. Both were too narrow. Life is larger, and strength livelier, than what they say.

Regularly, I would see Rodolphe, the young man with green eyes. He would come to visit me twice a week. He came after school, around five. We spoke little. He wouldn't say anything about my plaques. After making love, I would help him with his schoolwork. We would drink Italian red wine which I had delivered by the case. He did not ask any questions. I wouldn't question him either. His company was relatively pleasant to me. One night, I ordered him to scratch me. The excitation of my skin was at its peak. He was shy, then came closer to undress me. Finally he began rubbing my wounds gently. I muttered:

'Harder, harder, HARDER, HARDER . . .'

Then he began to finger me violently with one hand while flaying me frantically with the other. Blood was gathering under his nails . . . And pus on his fingers.

'To the left, to the right, higher, harder . . .'

The calves . . . I was exploding, the shock was building, a rough base shattering in my neurons, my nerves maddened . . . It was like a strange, yellow, crazy light before my eyes, freakish sobs began to break out, I was crying, my body was becoming too small, I wanted him to tear the sheath that oppressed me, this impossible limit, I needed space, air, freshness, I banged my head against the floor, in a muffled, dark sound, he was bearing down on me, driving into my belly over my sides, with a sort of rage in his eyes, which I could make out from under my open eyelids . . . My back stretched, my fingers useless, my breasts ploughed. He penetrated my skin and my sex all at once, pounding and scratching at the same time, flaying my wound from within my soft lips, tearing the skin with short and sharp blows. While imperceptibly losing control of his limbs, he went on bleeding me hard. He was taking pleasure in scraping into my rind, in driving headlong into the rift of the open belly, under the sex, above the bloodied skin, the flesh from below enmeshed with him beneath the membrane above, I was becoming crazed soft tissue, my veins without respite, my muscles assaulted by tremors, complexion dressed up in all colours . . . he operated in my deeper entrails, amputated my scales, worked my swollenness into glorious erections, my wounds, my defenceless fabric, lacerated by pleasure and joy . . . the shell pierced from all sides, and through all passageways . . . he was scalping me, grazing me, piercing me, perforating me, scraping my hide, searching the belly, stirring the depths, exploring the abyss of my cunt, trying to come to the end of my armour, the outside, the inside meeting suddenly, he beneath the skin, he above the rind, he was going all the way to the heart, from behind the drawn curtains of my bones, his finger in my mouth, then once more into the folds of my sexuality, my solemn velvet in contact with the tissues of the exterior, mixed fabrics, odd connections . . . he was untangling himself on my body, stripping my frame, from every-which recess . . . anatomy lesson, singular skin, nails, sweat and sperm, hacked ecstasies, the laughter of my eviscerated wounds . . . he was intruding through the skin, through my lips, bringing both the dark and the bright to the light, grandiose intimacy, opening of my nights, of my burrowed clearings, the nerves on which I danced, the immense pain, the supreme sting, the madness, the irritation before the killing, my liquid, bliss on pus, on blood, impatient comic obscenities, he was scoring the meat off me softly, all risks together, all the pearly pleasures . . . I was bursting like a laughter, I was stopping time, I was *vomiting* my difference.

Mehdi Belhaj Kacem

Anteform

Mehdi Belhaj Kacem

I woke up in the night; not having a watch any more, I picked up the phone to find out what time it was; I had planned, after leaving my dealer and in order to make the most of the full strength of the acid, to go to a rave taking place in a far Parisian suburb, which my dealer had told me about and had described the shuttle which would take me there; it was set in a grandiose abandoned steelworks plant, in which I arrived already in the perfect state, enlivened throughout all of my nerves, thanks to my preliminary ingestions, presenting myself perfectly *delivered* to the forces of the rave itself – {any area, whether it is climactic, elementary, intellectual, corporeal (however much it is always corporeal before anything else – it radiates, even if with extremely weak protons, throughout every other area) presents itself, when entered, as a silky but pervading *entwining* – not just because it is excessively folded and knotted back onto itself, but because it is in perpetual motion and evolution (any criterion (particularly of 'truth') that we use in judgment, in order to be formulated, must be dissociated from time and space as socially legislated; so that one's 'time' cannot be untangled without its criteria being untangled beforehand – and particularly so of our time, in which we have, more than ever, used the most untenable and fragile criteria in thinking) – effluvia and speeds, irrigations within the invisible pipings of these entwinings like an atmosphere filled with translucent candy floss – whirlwinding effects and occasional securing points – more or less solid recurrences, irrational points where the most unbelievable becomes possible

– frequencies of acceleration upon which one just glides, if not slides – or of deceleration and paralysis; when joining at least one of these currents in order to definitively wrench from it some profitable point, one that does not remain submerged and, as it were, bathed in the incubator of the atmosphere – a force, a dynamic that is unseizeable except at this one so easily, so quickly, removed point – you risk being snatched up by this or that speed coursing everywhere, filling space – and often being cast very far from the point originally sought; then, each of us is physically joined and in a few gulps, drained of our powers of movement, pulse, perception, speed of understanding)} – by this, I mean: delivered to the sensations which only the rave as such could supply – a line of force or of mutation (created by functions that alter the composition of the body thus mutated) which cannot be found anywhere but in this dynamic – and one cannot, in intellectual integrity, enter it sober and clear minded (disregarding that recent events implied I wouldn't ever be, whatever my condition, 'sober' or 'clear minded' any more) – at the risk of bathing, instead of in a rave, in a simple *projection* of one's own mind (as we do everywhere in daily life) – where everything would appear solely as the duplicate of all the principles, certainties, ready-made associations, processes, ordered reflexes that fill up thoughts; this head that was still mine, instead I wanted it pounded to the last degree, washed of its sap by the LSD blotter, torn and uprooted by glue sniffings – ultimately fanned and pulverised by long drawn-out puffs of Dutch Skunk – and immediately, my state of *stupefied availability* degenerated (but wasn't that the aim?) into an *unconditional offering* of the thinking-sensing alizari as *irascible* as an electric current, a self-offering to all the atmospheres available in the rave factory – it mutated, for it was the very celerity of this mutation – ignoring just as much where it came from as where it was going – a *dynamic* of mutations upon whose scattering, through whose complexity I was *dilacerated*, as if my flesh did not know which of these thousand threads to follow – and dissolving itself along each one of them, spread throughout the infinite intertwinings of their scatterings; I couldn't do much more, at that point, than stamp out a few very rough variations, but for the most part, I was sucked in by a *storm* – a barbed hurricane crackling through the entire site; my being snatched up was first confirmed by a kind of infinite prickling effected by the techno; my soma, *cleaved* along the length of its bark and *drained* into a thousand threads (*urchin*-body, dilacerated into straight threads of its flesh drained into the infinity of these threads, flesh melting then *bristling* up into the high roofs of the rave factory, and still *stretchable* – still drainable by the vampire space), released at each one of its pricklings (several per second) a small organic unity that fluttered about in the tiny interstices of these threads – a free *corpuscle*, fleeing, but soon re-intercepted by one or other of these thousand intertwined lines, to which this corpuscle added further intertwinings – but distributing themselves all over the room, they would soon resorb into the atmosphere's fiery but *entangled density* – so intense that it radioactivated what it drew down its thread, not that I had quite lost all my powers, for I could still feel them, but I couldn't at all, as expected, inflect any further the kinds of variations that were taking place; I had already been dancing for quite a while without having really decided to do so, instead being *hooked* by the merciless beat of the music – the continuous ligament set by the music imprisoning me just as it imprisoned anything within the music akin to melodic waverings or shiverings (however rapid), sonic flickerings (however rattled) – waves (waves because of their evanescence, perforated and exposed to their *fission* – to their *molecularity*, at once freed and disentegrated along these threads) – always surfacing in the tight vicinity of the rhythmical ligament – as if they couldn't have been conceived without its laced support everywhere; its omnipresence consti-tuted the one *link* to the hallucinated dancers; and just as the sonic colours had gone beyond this distention of dancing shadows and spirits that appear under milder drugs, swimming freely in the body as in an ethereal element – to become, in the conjunction of hallucinogens and music, *tadpoles* of minute sonic nuances, never released from the magnetic phlegm coating the rhythm, vaguely stirring and attempting a few strained flights before resor-bing into the semi-placental coating of the rhythmic stem – simi-larly, the dancers had been brutally taken hostage by the endless unfurling of the machinic pulse – sent into orbit, but in an extremely straight and channeled orbit, with an extremely binding consistency: similar in this respect to the drug-induced visions that had no choice but to conglomerate on the rhythm and encase themselves in it, the dancers through their dancing neither scared nor liberated anything, but increased the hold of the constricting rhythm on themselves, each step ceased being the attainment of a specific space and rhythm, but amounted to a further massing of bodies on the sole techno rhythm – all these bodies becoming nothing but a dense conglomeration tightly coagulated on the techno beat; not that it was unpleasant, nor had the drugs lost any of their euphoric or ecstatic powers, but the dancers' ecstasy and euphoria were becoming so regulated, vertebrated, by the techno rhythm, thereby almost familiar and unconscious, and thus, less appreciable as such – unlike those violent ecstasies produced by the same drugs in a more neutral context, and which are all the more powerful and demanding to the extent that they take away from those experiencing them all means of perception and sensation, so much so that at the very heart of ecstasy they have to invent a new language, new senses and a new thinking able to apprehend the astounding place in to which they are thrown – this cosmos where all is but fleeing, whirling and fluidity, requiring that the users design, to circumscribe these motions, their own marks to be able to enjoy the drugs' maximum intensity – contrary to the rave where everything was already arranged for the user to follow precisely marked-out tracks and to feel at home in this ecstasy, in other words, provided with all the supports, struts, prostheses, groundings upon which everything that may serve as body or thinking wouldn't have to make much effort to blend in; the rhythm, as it were, short-circuited the tremendous migrations and deportations of sense granted to the user by the drugs, in truth, it perforated everything with its reassuring beat, playing much the same role as the clock does for society or the pulse for the organism, it tyrannized everything with its pace and penetrated everywhere like a vertebrating tapeworm – I mean a tapeworm that wasn't only meant to be parasitic upon everything alive here, but also to vertebrate it, and to be parasitic to the very extent it was vertebrating it all the deeper: the whole body becoming the tight sheath of its hammering, close-fitting its consecutive moments down to the last shiver of a toe; so, the violence we had all felt when entering was none other than the violence of habituation – of the jailer setting the chains on the convict to the point of smothering him under their weight; this violence, ruling over all of us, also took the form of a hysterical mass-agglutination onto the techno ligament, a violence which, in the same way that it did not come from our own interior, but was ordered from the outside and injected therefrom into our arteries, would strive, as soon as it had taken hold in us, to *transcend* us, and to rejoin the rhythmic orb in a series of rapid loops: loops of vision, of enlivened and over-stretched colours, of sonic tumours quickly proliferating into enormous growls – and the individual, in thus anointing the techno ligament with all that his hallucinated mind and senses could conjure up, realized that he had become nothing but a means for the music to exist, and to exist only for its own sake through a whole transitive circuitry in which the dancer was but a point: for the first time in human history, music claimed its *independence* and achieved it, achieved its self-regulation and its exclusive self-enjoyment – no longer the means for humans to take over spaces other than the human one, but humans as a part, near-dispensable, in a set-up conceived by music to exist for itself; those very dancers, whose generalized dancing exuded a harmony less choreographic than bacterial, and indeed, each of us mattered as little as a bacteria: it was solely in our multiplicity that we could come to produce something like life, that of a moving, palpitating shower of particles, quite pleasant to see stirring around – but again, what was it that had spat us out and showered us into nature in this way, if not this divine rhythmic entity which ruled single-handedly over everything that existed here? I realized that in the hour since I'd arrived, I hadn't had any contact with anyone present, even if we had smiled to one another now and then in the course of the accelerations which the rhythm knowingly imposed the better to bind us together, but to bind us together as simple *particles* of rhythm: our smiles were nothing but the ecstatic waves created on the *surface* of the rhythmic flux – our smiles gaping as certain faces painted by a near-blind Goya gape: with the bliss of what believes itself to be human when in fact being no more than a speck of a crumbled husk, the husk of a black hole, or rather of a perforation that seems harmless at first, but eventually turns out to be afflicted by a dynamic spreading infinitely in every-which direction – the swallowing up of a black cosmos pretending to spare what it devours, only to swallow it all the better: the more it amplified, the more it had to grow around itself that human husk which sheathed it, increasingly disseminating us throughout space and imposing its amplification so much that we confused its force with our own, even though it was nothing but the pulverizing of what we were, our being sent into orbit, increasingly sifted, minuscule, dissolved into the galaxies: the result was a far too natural ecstasy, close to unconsciousness: we were in communion in the fullest sense of the word, and this communion had nothing to do with the rich and swarming solitudes of the mystics, but everything to do with the jaded crowding fomented by religions, only to end up slapping each one back all the more brutally into a glaring solitude: what brought us into communion and ecstasy was the very thing that in its stupendous growth scattered and dissolved us to feed its motion; everyone united in the ecstasy of rhythm, and not the least contact between us, only the pull of everything and everyone into the rhythm: in the same way that the sounds fluttered in tight spirals around the federating rhythm, nothing was left of us, in our pulses, our dances, our visions, our thoughts, our emotions, besides the emanations and *atomized spittles* of the rhythm, gravitating and floating all around – curling up around it like neon vines to which the rhythm's *magnetic seizure* effect never gave the slightest relief: the techno (called *trance*) particular to the room in which we were was also the most widely favoured, and for a second I wondered if it wouldn't be better to leave this one room to put to the test another kind of techno; with great effort and even sharp pain, I tore myself out of that atrociously placental rhythm, too placental to let me leave without exacting a harsh sanction: a whole network of nervous fibres, of materialized hallucinations, of multiple and freakish temporalities had taken root in me, and by leaving the room, I perpetrated the equivalent of a thousand brutal excisions – the faculties of my head and my soma were deployed to such a degree of intensity that in leaving the room, I was uprooting whole peoples and slaughtering many more yet, leaving behind mass graves of perceptions, sensations, thoughts; this mass organic treason literally made me the most degenerate body that ever was: I was disrupting in their very natures the fluids that ran in my nerves and neurons, and soon, I would be forced to upset all their functions and to wreak much extraction, mutilation and transplantation to put myself back into a shape such that I could simply *feel* the new climates I would be exposed to; like a smashed-up old car I drove on shaken by spasms of shame and by a strained effort to renew myself from deep inside; with the firm intention not to stop, I crossed the room where *ambient* techno prevailed, but my state couldn't prevent my body from absorbing, like an instant sponge, all the emissions that haunted this very calm section of the rave: indeed, the dancers were sleeping through this music more than dancing to it, they were sinking into it drowsily, as if into a stagnant pool whose putrefication exuded an exquisite and numbing scent: here, the mechanical production of happiness was brewed much more mildly than in the preceing room, the placental flooding was far more cottony and melliflous than under *trance*; an eternal cycle of blossoming was taking place here, swaddling the dancers under countless comfortable layers that would burst only to create a denser sheath of comforting: a bubble of heavy perfume would hatch from another bubble bursting noiselessly, nursing yet another bubble in which the dancer could curl up to give birth to a new bubble, even heavier and more intoxicating (but with a dozy rather than elated intoxication), to the point of being nothing but an unending succession of flaky and cosy places, successively hatched from within their innermost being; as for myself, I was overwhelmed by these increasingly suave and velvety, voluptuous, atmospheres; and relaxed by the caressing flows that twirled softly all about – but nevertheless, I managed to speed up a bit, slightly refreshed in fact, at the heart of this spellbinding warmth, by a draft coming from the third room, where something terrible resonated, something which seemed to be the *unholy* inflections of techno – I mean all the elements *inherent* to techno which it nonetheless strained to attenuate and sweeten down, if not altogether discard – particularly in this room whose breath was pulling at me commandingly; I went in, and the freshness I expected turned out to be an all-out attack: the rhythm was even faster than those preceding it, more explosive and more pressing in each surge of its incredible explosions – in a pounding of twenty or thirty blasts per second; and within this pounding, it was out of the question to discern anything like a rhythmic contour or core, for what claimed to be the rhythm was far too rapid for the human pulse to even consider finding its place or bearings in it: the tyranny of rhythm and pulse had been supplanted by an *antirhythmic* (and just as *antipulsive*) *terrorism*; with tremendous effectiveness: in the roar, one could detect the first of a vast machinery, with a mechanism as flawless as it was exclusive: I mean, all that remained were the cogs and wheels, the gears, the pulleys, the pistons of the apparatus churning full blast, without the least sonic embroidery or embellishment, and the machinery as a whole was thus taking the human pulse hostage to its motion, but now only for a few seconds, and not to intoxicate it but to detoxify it – and to detoxify it of itself: the music's grinding motion was too violent and too fast for the pulse to follow, obliging it to self-destruct in the momentum of this musical havoc, and from this havoc unknown pulsing lines were then born, lines that were not so much reproducing the stunning rhythm holding sway as liberated from any rhythmic habituation, and thus bobbing around, with perfectly free and harmonious variations, left to enjoy themselves with no support besides the unrelenting sabotage of all supports – unfathomably more ecstatic than any other techno-prompted ecstasy – and indeed such was, I suddenly realized, the main aim of *hardcore* techno (as it is called): not to infuse a tyrannical pulsing into the pulse, as *trance* would, not to provide the pulse with a space where it could enjoy itself in its most human expression, as does *ambient*, but to devise a rhythm and a machinery as infallible as possible, with an infallibility

unmatchable by any humanoid organism, so that their very per-
fection could open up, within their fascistic workings, disastrous
recesses in which any joint could crack with the sound of a
jack-hammered jaw, where any pulley could suddenly explode
and start to self-destruct into a perfect mechanical aberration,
where all kinds of implosions, crashes, collapses, blasts could
occur in the same way – and far from disrupting the overall
mechanism, would fully justify its design, testifying definitively,
under the fascistic surface, to the purely *anarchistic* nature of the
whole set-up: constantly threatening to break apart, it did not
break but on the contrary nourished itself with its anomalies,
collapses, unravellings; seizing on the human pulse to drive it to
its ultimate refuge, that is, to a great hyperfascistic pulsing – the
Mussolinian crowds started up their chants in your very blood-
stream, advancing in terrifying and overwhelming rows, with
raised banners and fists held high – the human drive was discovering the fascistic side of its nature, but pushed here to such
an extreme that it amounted to a deliberate sabotage of that very
drive – a monstrous carnage within the very ranks of the fascistic
atoms making up your blood, but which progressively opened
on to a formidable orgy, a barbaric onslaught that left you gasping, and jeopardized cardiac harmony, yet paving the way to an
even faster and purer breathing, more inebriating and musical
because it had forsworn any foundation or regulation, *uncovering*
the pulse that is *harboured* within the pulsing, the ecstatic oscilla-
tion that is usually concealed by the tempo of heartbeats: I was

one with these martial, industrial pulses, only to be all the freer to sabotage my pulse at its deepest level and to puncture these recesses of ecstasy which for the first time in the evening were really liberating me, my mouth wide open from slaughtering everything in my constitution, and to rebuild under the saturated nerves, the twisted viscera, the lacerated organs, the perforated neurons, a constitution made of oscillations and cracklings, of muffled advances and sudden accelerations, of effervescent reactions and deadstops that, themselves, were motions and reactions.

At the end of such a night, I finally felt excreted, exhausted, unnerved – *un-nerved*, that is emptied out, as if bared of my nerves exposed to the elements, taut and stretched to the critical point of their resistance; I walked towards the exit and, for the first time in a long while, felt overtaken by an *uncompromising void* – not the echo of a void, an exhaustion that would have brought me closer to the void, but the bloodlessness left by the repeated gashings of the body, as if daggered ceaselessly, no matter the circumstances I had been in during the last months – a void with neither end nor edges, but with no movement or breathing either, a dispossession which the most alienated of the alienated could hardly begin to imagine; I would have run as fast as I could if only I had thought or willed it – if I had possessed the notions of willing and running – but all I knew to do was walk with fluffy legs and dangling arms, hollow-headed and my tongue slightly out, its tip barely skimming the rim of my lips; I have no recollection of the route taken from the exit of the rave to my mattress, on to which I fell in a slumber that was to last eighteen hours (and maybe, my dismal health of that winter of '95–'96 was but the very natural *hibernating instinct* of the grizzly bear) – and it was weeks before I could understand what had happened to me.

Frédéric Beigbeder

Trashed

Frédéric Beigbeder

What can you offer a generation that grows up to discover rain's poisoned and sex leads to death?

Guns 'n' Roses

Midnight. Girls half-naked. Marc half-wrecked. The frenzy's at its height. The universe is a starry chaos in motion, a psychedelic sea of confetti. An acid-sirtaki goes on for half an hour without a break.

Marc wanders from bar to dancefloor and back. The Lobotomies he's drunk are working on his system. He communes telepathically with the thumping infra-bass. Joss knows just how to get clubbers under the hypnotic influence. It looks like he's going to be at his best ever tonight – performing live, no safety-net. He mixes from six turntables simultaneously: Zorba the Greek, techno-trance, a quivering of violins, Andean pipes, a clatter of typewriters, Duras and Godard in conversation. Tomorrow: nothing left of it all. To intensify the vibe, Fab is handing out whistles.

The dance loses itself in a series of black-outs and resurrections. The dance is a looping evanescence, a delirious philosophy, a theory of complexity. The dance is Back. A whirligig of digital horses on a rogue carousel. A circle has formed. People put hands on each other's shoulders. Everything's spinning round. Only one thing is certain: the girls have extra tits. Marc closes his eyes to block them out and the multi-coloured blotches of light make him ten times dizzier. All these girls stark naked under their clothes! Gorgeous navels, delectable sinews, cheeky noses, delicate necks ... The possibility that these Bright Young Things in their stretch-tight little black dresses, these flighty creatures with fringes veiling their eyes might happen to exist has deterred him all his life from leaping into the void.

They generally have first names ending in *a*. Their interminable eyelashes curve like ski-jumps. When you ask how old they are, they reply 'twenty' as if it were of no importance. They must suspect that their age is the sexiest thing about them. They've never heard of Marc Marronnier. He'll have to lie, stroke a hand or two, take an interest in International Relations, do whatever's necessary. They've grown up too quickly; don't yet know the secret codes. They'll fall right into the trap. They'll absent-mindedly suck a thumb while listening to him quote Paul Léautaud. It won't take much to impress them. Yes, Marc knows Eric Cantona and Gérard Depardieu. Yes, he's been on Dechavanne's TV show, and Christine Bravo's. For such prey as this, to hell with his principles, he'll forget about Name-Forgetting.

Maybe, just when he least expects it, one of them will brush her lips lightly against his and invite him back to her designer garret. Will he go? Will he kiss her neck in the taxi? Will he come in his trousers in the stairwell? Will there be a Lenny Kravitz poster pinned up over the bed? How many times will they make love? Will she fall asleep on him, for God's sake? Finding the latest Nicholas Evans novel on the bedside table, will Marc be able to restrain himself from running away as fast as he can?

He opens his eyes. Ondine Quinsac, the famous photographer, is getting bored on champagne and a cluster of gigolos, who are being given a gentle brush-off. Some recycled demi-mondaines are playing at being hermaphrodite, so as to remain demi-something, no doubt. Henry Chinaski puts his hand on Gustav von Aschenbach's arse; Aschenbach makes no protest. Jean-Baptiste Grenouille sniffs Audrey Horne's armpits. Antoine Doinel takes a swig from senile-delinquent-on-duty Consul Geoffrey Firmin's bottle of mescal. And the Hardissons play rugby with their baby. (The untried Patrick Bateman converts the try.)

The combination of Latin-American cocktails and Parisian puns is a heady one: it takes all sorts to make or break a world.

Suddenly, the lights go down and the strains of a classic track float over this degenerate set. It's Ella and Louis: 'Summertime'. Joss announces fifteen minutes of Ladies' Choice over the mike. Marc takes the opportunity to accost Ondine Quinsac.

'It's Ladies' Choice, so I'm inviting you to invite me to dance.'

The photographer is encircled every which way: by young bores gathered round her and by rings under her darkly shadowed eyes. She looks him up and down.

'I accept, on account of "Summertime", my favourite song. And because . . . you look a bit like William Hurt, only naffer.'

She wraps her arms round him and murmurs the lyrics in a husky voice, staring him straight in the eyes.

'Oooh, your daddy's rich and your ma is good-looking/So, hush little baby, baby don't you cry . . .'

From so close, Marc can read her thoughts. Thirty-seven, no kids, she's been on a diet for six months, can't give up smoking (hence the gravelly voice), is allergic to sunshine, plasters on foundation and an ineffectual concealer for the rings under her eyes. Her infertility depresses her and her depression moves him.

'So,' he says, 'I'm dancing a slow with the hottest photographer in town. You wouldn't like to hire me as a top model?'

'Oh no, you're too skinny. You need to do some exercise, then come and see me. Besides, something tells me fashion's not your thing. You look so healthy, so normal . . .'

'So hetero . . . so ordinary . . . Go on, insult me!'

Have we already mentioned Marc's braying laughter – a tremendous, uncontrollable, maddening noise – that he bursts into at all his own jokes? Well, now you know. Hey, Joss has changed the record.

'Hey, Joss has changed the record,' says Ondine. 'Another slow. Is this Elton John?'

'Yes, "Candle in the Wind", a hymn to Marilyn Monroe, the Alma tunnel, and Hollywood lighting technology. Am I invited to dance again?'

Ondine nods.

'I suppose I don't have any choice.'

'That's right: if you'd refused, I'd have written in all the papers that you were a dyke.'

Forty-year-old women turn Marc on. They have every-thing: experience and enthusiasm. Both whorehouse madams and frightened virgins. They're so amazed to have a chance to teach you everything!

'You're a friend of Joss Dumoulin's?'

'There was a time when we used to go out drinking together a fair bit, which establishes a bond. That came to an end in Tokyo, five years ago.'

'I'd like to do his portrait. Right now I'm putting together an exhibition of portraits of celebrities suspended on a pulley, with condensed milk on their cheeks. Could you talk to him about it?'

'I guess he's bound to be interested in such a wonderful project. But *why* are you doing it?'

'The show? Oh, it's to illustrate the close relationship between photography, sexuality and death – that's the concept, in a nutshell.'

Marc jots down on one of his Post-Its: 'Demonstration of the Three Whys axiom sometimes only requires one Why, when the subject of the experiment has a drawn face, is reserved by nature, and wears a tulle dress.'

Ladies' Choice is about to end. Fab is dancing a slow sandwiched between Irène de Kazatchok and Loulou Zibeline. Clio has woken up to ask castrato-voiced man-of-leisure and heir-to-a-fortune William K. Tarsis III to dance, only to fall asleep again on his shoulder. Her lower lip trembles in the yellow spotlights. Ari, a mate of Marc's (a designer of video games for Sega), comes up to annoy him.

'Watch it! Ondine's an ultraviolent nympho!'

'I know. Why do you think I asked her to dance?'

'I'm not letting you get away with that!' protests the photographer. 'I'm the one who asked you to dance, not the other way round.'

Ari looks like a Bronx-born Luis Mariano. He carries on dancing beside them. As soon as Joss announces that Ladies' Choice is over, Ari pounces on Ondine.

'Right, my turn now! You can't refuse!'

Marc is not possessive enough and far too much of a coward to complain. The photographer's face remains blank, expressionless, with vacant eyes. If she's putting on an act, she deserves an Oscar for Best Show of Indifference.

'Nice meeting you,' Marc says casually, leaving them without a backward glance.

No doubt Ari and Ondine have already forgotten him. At parties, nothing should last more than five minutes: neither conversations nor people. Otherwise, run a risk worse than death: boredom.

Upstairs, Clio is freaking out big time. There must be some Euphoria left in her veins. Imagine Gwyneth Paltrow in a latex dress in a remake of *The Exorcist* and you get a rough idea of the scene. She's attracting an audience. She shouts, 'I love you', squeezing champagne flutes until the glass shatters. Her hands bubble with blood and splinters of glass, her palms for ever lost to the palm-reader's art.

'ALOOONE! ALONE! ALOOONE!'

Seeing Joss's expression and that of his new friend, the PR trendy beside him, Marc realises that Clio must have caught them both in the DJ booth choosing the next record, down on all fours or something. He says to Clio:

'Dumoulin's had enough? He's given you the push? Never mind, I'm your dreams come true! When do we fuck?'

'No, thanks. I've given up,' sniffs Clio.

He then grabs a bottle of Jack Daniels and pours it over her hands to disinfect them (Marc only just failed to get his first aid certificate). Clio's screams drown out the 10,000 watt sound system for at least twelve seconds. She delivers a pretty exhaustive list of English swearwords, then dries her tears. The onlookers disperse, and so it is that Marc comes to be trailing Clio in his wake for the second time, holding her by her delicate, bare wrist.

Music: the Beloved's 'Sweet Harmony':

Let's come together
Right now
Oh yeah
In sweet harmony
Let's come together
Right now

Oh yeah
In sweet harmony
Let's come together
Right now
Oh yeah
In sweet harmony
Let's come together
Right now
Oh yeah
In sweet harmony

Got it all worked out.

They sit on a sofa, with Clio's hand under a beam of light, and Marc tries to pick out the fragments of shattered glass one by one.

'Marc, I'm thirsty,' wails the spaced-out supermodel between moans.

'No! No more messing about!'

'Can I drink out of your glass?'

She eyes his Lobotomy on the rocks.

'Are you crazy? I daren't imagine what'd happen if you mixed that with . . .' (Marc bites his tongue: he remembers that he spiked her drink earlier *without her knowing*.) 'Well, OK . . . If you insist, I'll fetch you a glass of water.'

And he gets up, cursing under his breath the scientific advances in pharmacology.

Ondine Quinsac is lying on the bar, her tulle dress pulled up. Ari has covered her with whipped cream and is licking her with the help of some obliging friends. This holds up the barman. Which is why it takes Marc a good fifteen minutes to obtain the glass of water and the bandage the young model so urgently needs.

When he gets back, licking his lips, Clio is just finishing off his Lobotomy. She smiles at him and falls asleep, singing. Consternation and dismay. Marc sighs and, drinking the glass of water, bandages her hands. He's not sure of anything any more. He no longer believes in anything – and he's not even sure of that. He should talk to her, but he keeps his trap shut. Silence is fool's gold.

The photographer covered with whipped cream is now being collectively screwed. One guy in front, another on top, Ari behind. A model of efficiency in terms of time and motion.

(If Marc doesn't do something very soon, Clio will die of an overdose in his lap: a mixture of alcohol and ecstasy in mega quantities can send the heart into overdrive.)

Feeling a rising inspiration, he takes out his Post-It notes and writes down these lines:

> *Wanting ever so much to be bad,*
> *She was ever so scantily clad.*
> *After catching a chill,*
> *She's a virgin still . . .*
> *Sneezing's a turn-off. So sad.*

(On the sofa, Clio is foaming at the mouth, her eyeballs have rolled back, her face is drained of colour.)

Marc is pleased with his poem. Perfect.

(Clio's heart is beating fit to burst.)

To recap: Marc's score so far is none too brilliant. An aged hackette buttonholed him during dinner, and the girl sitting next to him on the other side is now Fab's. He couldn't rise to the challenge of the PR nymphette who was his for the taking – she's now cavorting with the superstar-DJ. As for the forty-something depressive he danced two slows with, half the party is currently fucking her on the bar.

(Clio is grinding her teeth, white froth lines the corners of her mouth.)

The only chick Marc's left with, poor Clio, is mashed to oblivion.

(Clio has appalling cramps in her legs which, in her destroyed state, she can't even feel.)

And Joss has just dumped the Clio in question like a used condom.

(Clio's temperature varies between 36 and 43 degrees centigrade.)

Truth is, the only shag Marc could get is well out of it, and in any case no way would he hit on a mate's ex.

(Clio's body is racked with cold sweats.)

Seriously, Marc, your attitude sucks.

(Clio's guts are in fast spin.)

And what a dumb chat-up line: 'Can I offer you a lemon-
ade?' Marronnier, you're a fuckwit.

(Clio's electro-encephalogram is practically a straight line.)

Shit, this chick Clio weighs a ton!

(Clio's pulse stops beating. The End: clinical death.)

Marc looks at her latex dress, her white back, her gaunt
face . . . She's got a weird expression . . . There's a word for it,
a very *fin-de-siècle* word: a warped expression. With her bandaged
hands, her stomach full of acid and alcohol, she emanates an
unwholesome charm. Her long hair is spread out on the sofa.
She looks like a decadent goddess. Even her body looks warped.
Marc feels sorry for her. He bends over to kiss her, but since
she's lying in his lap her body pushes into his stomach every
time he leans over. As he kisses Clio, he blows air into her lungs.
She eventually revives, of course.

At the centre of the world (club privé, Le Crap, in Paris, towards
the end of the second millennium AD, shortly before 1 a.m.), a
young poser has just saved the life of a numbed-out young lady.
No one realises it, not even them. Maybe, at that hour, God
hasn't yet crashed out.

Éric Faye

Dinner with the Zeuses

Éric Faye

'**Up there,**' **cries Poseidon,** out of breath.

'I hope you know what you're saying,' says Hermes, ten metres further downhill, sweating as he picks his way through the rocks with the help of his wingèd staff. 'What's the idea of Zeus leaving home and settling so much higher up?'

'Zeus was worried about intruders, and loss of privacy. He tells me that men have built a refuge close by the top of Olympus, and more and more of them are making the climb in summer. You know how the Old One is; he's not too fond of men, and things won't get any better.'

'To be fair, it has to be said . . .'

Hermes and Poseidon reach a steep slope, a few dozen metres below the big villa. They sit down, panting, and catch their breath. 'How cold it is,' sighs Hermes. 'I'm used to hard travelling and rough country, but here . . . Isn't that Hera on the front steps? I hope she's in a good mood.'

'That's her, indeed. She's aged.'

'They say that with Zeus it's even worse.'

'Ageing, when you're immortal, is dreadful. But considering our destiny, how can we stay immune? Even Apollo and Aphrodite are showing signs of wrinkles, so I hear.'

Hermes and Poseidon push at a gate, which creaks as it swings open. Now they're in the grounds of the villa. 'What a handsome building,' says Poseidon. 'Think of the tonnage, if it was a ship . . .' Hera waves at them. A black dog races towards them, barking as it comes; Hera calls sharply: 'Cerberus, down! Good dog.'

'Hades is here already,' sighs Hermes. 'He won't have changed, not he. Punctual to the second, and can't make a move without that damned hound.'

Hermes and Poseidon greet Hera with kisses and enter the hall. 'Hello, Hera,' says Poseidon. 'Good to see you again.'

Hermes forces a smile. 'I do hope that we aren't the last to arrive. How pleasant it is up here, Hera.'

Poseidon exclaims at the colonnades and frescoed walls, and turns admiringly towards the goddess. 'What made you move here?'

'Another of Zeus's ideas. We just couldn't bear it any more, on Olympus. He moped all day long, it got me down. Olympus kept reminding him of the good old days when people believed in him – I mean, believed in us. Then he thought about these mountains, still uninhabited. We're actually located on the peak where Prometheus was chained . . .'

'Dear Prometheus,' Hermes cuts in. 'If it hadn't been for him making the gift of fire to men, they might show more respect for us today.'

'Don't let's harp on that old story again,' says Hera. 'Come on inside. You'll have some nectar to warm you up? We'll serve the ambrosia when everybody's here. Follow me.'

'Nectar,' sighs Hermes. 'It's an age since I've had any. Before, when I was out on my rounds, there'd always be a nip waiting for me . . .' He reaches for a goblet and continues: 'But where is the Old One?'

'He's in a really filthy mood. He skulks in his study and won't see anyone, not even Athena. He blames Christ. These days, we can't take that kind of competition.'

A knock at the gate, and enter Apollo and Ares, followed by Pallas Athena. They have all taken the aerial route. They enthuse about the site and the villa. 'Hera, what a marvellous idea to meet again as we did in the good old days. You live like hermits.' Is it Ares who declaims, Apollo who coos? Both have their mouths ostentatiously open, and a glint in their eyes. They turn in unison towards Hermes and Poseidon, as if they have just this minute noticed them. 'I say. Who have we here?' But Hera intervenes. 'Come in, do come in. Zeus won't be long. Anyway, I don't think we're expecting anyone else. Hephaestus has sent his apologies. There's an eruption in the Philippines. Dionysus and Demeter have harvests to attend to, Aeolus a typhoon in Cipango, so . . .'

'And what about Hades? That was Cerberus who went for us out there, wasn't it?'

'Hades?' (Hera gives a sudden shudder.) 'Yes, he's here. It's Hades that the Old One has been closeted with for the last hour. He'll tell you about it himself.'

'Hera, you're hiding something from us.'

'The truth is that Zeus is very depressed. Nobody worships him any more. All day long he mulls it over, broods on it, rehearses it, time and time again: can you still proclaim yourself a god if no one believes in you, if the people at your feet deny that your feet even exist?'

'Ah,' growls Ares, 'a crisis of identity. We've all been through that one, off and on. And he's not doing anything about it?'

'What do you suggest? There's no psychiatrist for depressive gods. No offerings for two thousand years . . . not a single sacrifice. And all the shrines in ruins, trampled by tourists, mauled by archaeologists . . .'

'What about thunder? Thunderbolts?'

'Occasionally, yes . . . he still throws a bolt from the blue. But do you think it reminds them of Zeus, down there? Nowadays they explain everything in terms of their so-called scientific phenomena. You, Apollo, with your plague-bearing arrows, do you believe the humans connect them with your power of destruction? Or Vulcan with his eruptions? Or you, Ares, with wars?'

'No one mentions us any more except in school textbooks and tourist guides to Greece. It's a disgrace. Allah is showing off right now, preening himself over the new markets won in Africa and Asia, but he'll smile on the other side of his face if by the end of the next millennium he's mentioned only in books about Arabia!'

'The Old One tries hard to make the best of it, I assure you,' Hera breaks in.

'My Nordic colleague, Tyr, is in despair,' Ares pursues. 'The nations that used to revere him have become the most peaceful people on the planet. He told me they make contributions to – hang on, what was it? – oh I have it, peace-keeping forces. It's the world turned upside-down . . .'

'At least, you, with your Mediterranean countries, Ares . . .'

'Oh, please. Nothing substantial now for fifty years. The best weapons never leave the arsenals. They make them, store them, then pass decrees to ban them. It's enough to make you tear your hair out . . . Not even the Greeks cross swords any more. From time to time, a squall brews up with the Turks, but then it all blows over again. All they do, each summer, is allow their lands to be vandalised by barbarian hordes. I feel ashamed.'

Poseidon speaks up: 'Men have replaced us with governments. Navy Minister here, Defence Minister, Agricultural Minister there . . . They're always in the public eye, swanning around, riding the skies like you, Athena, with your golden sandals. They have wings of steel, and move as speedily as you do. And when the humans lose patience with their ministers, they replace them! That's their advantage over us! Disposable deities, who curry favour with their believers. Yes, the world turned upside-down. So we, of course . . . But what can Zeus and Hades be cooking up together?'

'I told you he was very depressed,' Hera replies. 'Take yesterday: another false alarm. He thought a revival had started, a straw in the wind – you know how he raises his hopes. It was only a film-shoot about the Trojan war – or was it the fall of Sparta? – anyway, nothing serious, just play-acting, cardboard walls.'

'So . . . ?'

'So then he summoned Aeolus, who blew it all away with a tornado, ravaged the set in seconds. They're making fun of us, he said. If there was a law court for gods to sue gods, he'd bring cases against Allah and Jehovah and sue for aggravated damages. Wait, though . . . I think I hear them coming.'

Zeus appears in the main hall through the archway at the far end, together with Hades, and Charon the ferryman. Cerberus accompanies them, wheezing, slavering copiously from all three lolling tongues: old age.

'My friends!' exclaims the father of the gods. 'Sons, brothers . . . Thank you for accepting my invitation. You won't be sur-prised when I tell you that I have not asked you here merely to sup nectar and nibble at grapes. I have something important to divulge. Something that wrings my heart. For how many cen-turies have we waited for a sign from men? Only last week I was at Baal's home with Thor: they too are at the end of their tether. After disowning us, men turned to new deities, a second, more superficial, degenerate generation, with a god for each continent, a god of all trades, as if one could be an expert in every field, as if, for instance, you, Ares, knew all about winds and harvests and could stand in for Aeolus or Demeter any day, at a moment's notice . . . I used to hope for something to crop up, some spark to fly, but wherever we consult them the oracles are against us, my sons and brothers. More than two thousand years have elapsed since we were forsaken, and men have a dwindling belief, so it seems, in the worth of the gods. One by one, they are discarding them. Less and less do men set foot in those temples where once they used to worship them. We might rejoice in that, if it worked in our favour, but no such thing. And now, men have acquired a power still greater than my thunderbolts: the power to destroy their own race. Yes, I see you smiling, you feel a twinge of hope. What the Old One has failed to achieve, men themselves will achieve on their own. But if they do, Poseidon, then it will be at the expense of the waves, of the winds and storms that Aeolus unleashes, the harvests that Demeter oversees . . . This Earth will be a desert, burned to cinders, an uninhabitable world that we will have to abandon. For where? For what? Men have pushed us to the crossroads . . .'

'I wanted to tell you that I am weary of all this,' he resumed after a silence. 'Though I drink draught upon draught of nepenthe, that potion which should bring on forgetfulness of sorrows, it all revives too quickly in my memory. I can't expel men from my mind: they haunt me by day and plague me in my nightmares. And worse than that, they frighten me more and more often, I must admit . . . I read in your faces that you, my sons and brothers, are close to sharing my view . . . So I come to what I wanted to announce to you: I have decided to leave this villa.

Not to find a new one on a more inviolate peak where the air bites colder still, no . . . I believe that the gods no longer belong among the peaks. It's an alternative Olympus we require, a palace in the bowels of the Earth . . . A shelter from men's madness, a chance to survive them. I their father . . . They no longer know how to use fire. Day after day, they play with it. Helios, if you were here, you would understand that they will end by turning the Earth into a ball of fire like the Sun. I'm sure of it. What did I do on the day I created them? Fool that I was! We were so happy, warring among ourselves, with the Titans, the demigods . . . Hades, my brother, speak in my stead, I'm worn out. I no longer have the courage to go on, and words fail me. So explain to everybody that you are going to welcome me to a suite in your underworld, and I mean to withdraw there for the remainder of eternity. As for you, Charon the ferryman, make ready your boat.'

Vincent Ravalec

Black-Magic Nostalgia

The sun had disappeared for good and the gargoyles on the cathedral were starting to move, gargoyles whispering and rustling with an irritable murmur, and I'm thinking that we should have an umbrella or a hat or at least something to protect us from the downpour – an oilskin or an anorak, an anorak would be good, they make fur-lined ones now, waterproof on the outside, fur-lined on the inside, I've an idea that there are even some on special offer. Their fat, bulging eyes carved out of the limestone blinked in the dim light. Not long ago the church authorities had ordered that the cathedral be completely renovated but as soon as the scaffolding came down, the walls had turned black again and while some people had blamed pollution and cars – all those cars and factory smoke, one day they'll catch up with all of us – others had greeted this turn of events with curses, saying that the Archbishop was at fault and that it was obviously a sign that religion had well and truly failed. An evening paper had even run the headline, OUR LADY OF DAMNATION, implying that maybe the Devil, or at least some suspect force, was behind the whole thing.

It had been raining now for thirty days and thirty-three nights and Marianne had just told me that she was pregnant.

At first, the heat was the worst problem. There'd been an unprecedented drought since the start of spring, but feeling hot in summer is not the cruellest of punishments and when people realised that they were still paddling in the fountains in October, half-naked, and still enjoying the holidays that seemed to be never-ending, at that precise moment you wouldn't have found many people complaining.

It was just afterwards that the sky had grown dark and the rain had started – 1 November, All Saints' Day.

Clouds had massed in the west, a whiteish veil had seemed to cover the horizon, and then the first drops had fallen, welcomed with shouts of joy, and the whole city had ended up dancing in the streets, celebrating the return of water and the end of drought. The rain hadn't stopped since.

'Are you going out?' Marianne had asked me. 'Did you see they've found more snakes in the Métro?'

The child was an idea which had been in the air for a while. I had vaguely gone with it, hoping that time would solve this potential problem, a child suddenly being dropped into the middle of this whole fucking mess: you'd have to have lost all grasp on reality to take that sort of proposition on board, but unfortunately it had ended up becoming a real issue.

'They're bound to be ones that have escaped from Quai de la Mégisserie,' I had explained gently. 'It's not as if we're in the jungle, you know. We are in Paris.'

I put my things in a little bag, the same little bag I took with me when I went to work, told Marianne not to worry and left before she had time to get started on Pharaoh and the rods turning into serpents. This whole subject of the baby had shed a different light on the current state of affairs, a solemn, significant one that I only half-liked.

Vincent Ravalec

The janitor was watching the rain fall with some other people from the building. When I walked past he said it's still not stopping, and I went, no, you're right.

Recently, I had painted a tiny church, a really sweet one surrounded by incense smoke and the sort of organ music which makes space seem heavy and immaterial at the same time – a miniature church which you could have used as a dolls' house. In the sky I'd added medieval hang-gliders which suggested vaguely malevolent birds. 'Are you coming back late?' Marianne shouted through the window. 'Look after yourself, take care.'

Although not precarious, our situation couldn't have been described as exactly stable, and we were both getting by on our wits. Marianne got clients through Minitel, guys who wanted to be tied up and whipped and, according to her, generally nothing else: not really a working girl, just a few goes with the strap and a pair of handcuffs three afternoons a week. The rest of the time she'd wander around the flat, busy with her mysterious preparations or smoking cigarettes, all of it, more or less, having something to do with a dance performance, a piece for which she was making strange costumes, the Fool with Two Faces, the Old Demoness and the Cormorant King being the main characters.

I, meanwhile, fancied myself as a painter and ripped off old people. Poor, old people I picked out at random from museums, guided tours or public gardens and then conned them by explaining that I wasn't from Paris, I'd come to town on the strength of a small ad to go into partnership in a fruit and vegetable business and ended up losing everything to a bunch of unscrupulous crooks. As a rule, old people are bored and they're happy with any old rubbish.

Outside, the street looked like a desolate landscape interpreted by a modern artist. Since the start of the week, tarpaulins had begun to appear on cars – different coloured ones: pink, apple green, violet, transparent – and they gave the whole scene a distinctive atmosphere, a flicker of imagination in the midst of the most dismal surroundings: a not particularly attractive and half-flooded Parisian street, a grey day at the start of what was perhaps a new end of the world and, scattered about, multicoloured conceptual packaging. I picked up my car which luckily still started and set off on my latest venture: to rob some recent acquaintances – grannies and grandads in the west of Paris – of their fat little nest eggs.

Did we have the ideal set-up to welcome on earth a new being, a young life waiting to blossom? I wasn't convinced. To tell the truth, I could have tried to make money out of my painting or get a job as an illustrator, but I had a certain reluctance to establish on-going relationships with my contemporaries, so, other than when I was forced to, I preferred to keep my distance. Besides, I had the feeling that the slightest mercenary undertaking would irredeemably taint my artistic drive. I always thought of rock paintings and their particular charm, buried deep in caves, waiting in total darkness for millennia and yet displaying a power and a vitality

———

that would be hard to match. Painting for me was an almost magical act, just short of the point where witchcraft starts, and totally incompatible with even the slightest form of commerce.

For the time being, the thought of everything unravelling left me pretty cold. I was taking care of my business: the old people, the paintings and the curious task I'd set myself to compile a definitive record of the mystery of the cathedrals and the esoteric meaning of the Great Work. Unlike Marianne, I didn't have a fear of death to keep at bay the whole time.

The traffic hadn't died down that much. The flooding was becoming dangerously heavy, so they'd decided to cut off the electricity and have another go at making the grid watertight. The city was going to be plunged into a total blackout until the next morning: nothing but blackness, rain and the reflection of headlights in the water. If all went well, by morning I'd be in a position to decide about this problem of the child with a completely clear head.

The media had been broadcasting information for several days, posters had been stuck up more or less everywhere asking people to stay at home, and a sort of curfew had been declared. There was almost no one to be seen on the streets, except for a few people hurrying along, late getting home, and columns of National Electricity Board trucks, backed up by the army, driving slowly towards key intersections, creating – as if it wasn't palpable enough already – a terrible sense of death, war, and of living under a state of emergency.

The old people lived on a sort of estate – not that big, just two buildings next to each other – a jointly owned retirement complex where the occupants were savouring the comfortable rewards of a lifetime's labour. At the first sign of unrest no doubt they'd rushed to withdraw all their savings, and the announcement of a blackout would have convinced any who'd held back. According to my calculations, their stash must be approaching its optimal size.

I drove through the ghostly city towards Saint-Cloud bridge. I'd filled up with petrol that afternoon and the back of the car was loaded up with the equipment I needed for my enterprise.

Just before the Bois de Boulogne a roadblock forced me to slow down. Men in oilskins were waving luminous batons and when I stopped, one of them swore that it was bloody antisocial not to observe the curfew, they had enough problems with the rain as it was. I told him that my wife had just given birth and I was racing to the happy event without giving a thought – I hoped they'd understand – to this whole blackout business. They let me through, grumbling, and just as I started up the engine, I caught sight of someone standing slightly back, dressed in an oilskin as well, and, for a brief second, the figure's face was lit up by the glare of my headlights, leaving me stunned, as if a powerful electric shock had passed right through me. The figure had smiled at me, a friendly, slightly sad smile and it was a face I knew, the face of a girl who'd died a few years before and whose funeral I'd gone to.

Vincent Ravalec

My jaw was numb. My God, I tried to murmur, my God what are you doing here, but before I had time to rush towards her and clear the whole thing up, the figure drew back into the darkness and the men behind me shouted at me to drive on, hey are you going to move or what, and I drove away, my trembling hands gripping the wheel while I repeated that I must have seen wrong, it had to be a mistake.

The next thing I knew, I was approaching my destination and I had to concentrate on what I was doing and shake off this terrifying feeling that I'd met a dead person in the flesh.

My timing was worked out to the last second and I immediately got down to work. The same thoughts kept going round in my mind: bringing a child into the world was a serious decision, it wasn't the sort you take lightly: if you thought about it objectively, it was an absolutely horrific decision. There were moments when the only clear thoughts that emerged were that the world was done for, no hope at all, and wanting to perpetuate this grim farce would make the curse hanging over our heads worse and add to the weight of our sins, and, in so doing, to the weight of the burdens awaiting us in the future. The only objective reason was to please Marianne. I knew she was sick of all that Minitel business. The simplest most self-evident way to give a new meaning to her existence was, of course, a pretty little doll that would allow her at last to fulfil her destiny as a woman: becoming a mother.

I cut the motor just before the entrance to the car park and

---

freewheeled into the middle of the courtyard. They'd turned a car port into a vault with a cavity wall of breeze blocks and a security door. First I neutralised the exits with padlocks so that no one could get out, and then I broke down the door to the cellars. There was a risk that doing this would make a noise but I'd prepared for that and my plan covered such imponderables as the psychology of my victims. These people had a strong propensity to believe in the supernatural, so I'd worked out a show geared to their taste for the esoteric.

I'd put on my combat gear: tight-fitting black overalls with a phosphorescent skeleton printed on them, a helmet with antlers – Marianne had been involved in some stupid play the winter before – and thick ski goggles to complete the picture. The noise would inevitably bring the bravest ones running out and I didn't fancy having to resort to violence or threats, so I'd set up a battery-powered ghetto-blaster to play horrible music – abstract music that made the hairs on your head stand on end – plus a few flares and me coming through the fireworks as a skeleton: there was no chance they'd try to have a go at me.

At last, before your very eyes, the invisible makes its appearance, ha, ha! I must admit that sometimes my ingenuity terrified me.

I finished breaking down the door to the cellars. It was zero hour two, and the only sound was the plop, plop of the rain bouncing off the Plexiglas roof of the bike shelter.

The picture I was in the middle of painting at the time portrayed a sort of hybrid being, half-man, half-woman, at the entrance to an immense labyrinth – Theseus facing his destiny – and that was exactly the feeling I had that evening, standing in front of the gaping hole of the basement, rigged out in a strange costume and a horned helmet, having travelled through a flooded city deprived, on a moonless night, of the slightest glimmer of light, a feeling that a number of paths were opening up in front of me but that, when all was said and done, only one of them would be the right one. All my gear was on a little trolley I'd stolen that afternoon from near a building site, I felt calm, concentrated on my work, my mind free of the slightest scruple. I pushed my makeshift shopping trolley in front of me and went into the cavern.

Quick as a flash, I set up on the mezzanine some large mirrors which I'd found on previous visits. I positioned them to reflect the torches of any potential troublemakers and confuse them even more. Then I pressed Play on the tape recorder. It let out a terrible wail, compared to which the worst contemporary music seemed a model of harmony, and I started smashing in the breeze blocks of the cavity wall with a sledgehammer. The telephones weren't working either that night . . .

Ilan Duran Cohen

Wonderland

My mother's on the phone. She's very worried. She says my father locked himself in the bathroom. He didn't turn on the light. He just stayed there, motionless in the dark. She waited by the door, not saying anything. When he came out, his eyes were red. She thinks he'd been crying. She doesn't know why. Do I have any idea? What's wrong with my father?

She'd like to know why everything seems to be moving away from her. She feels that people are refusing to talk to her. She wants me to tell her something, it doesn't matter what, as long as I talk to her. So I try to provoke her because she likes to be provoked. Only by me.

'Why did you have me circumcised?'

She's silent. She's surprised, of course. She wanted me to tell her about New York and I'm talking about my dick.

'What are you talking about?'

'Why did you have me circumcised?'

'Because! That's the way it is. You're Jewish! I mean, really, of all the stupid questions! How's your sister?'

'What difference would it have made? Tell me!'

'It's cleaner. I don't know! That's the way it is. It's not the sort of thing you argue about. What's got into you? Are you ashamed to be Jewish? We send you to live in New York and now you're ashamed to be Jewish!'

My mother doesn't like reassessments. She's decided to be

happy, and that's all there is to it. Her happiness is us. That's the way it is. It won't change. It mustn't change.

'What got into him to make him go and lock himself in the bathroom, in the dark? He didn't even take the trouble to run the tap to make it seem like he was washing. He worries me, your father. He could have gone into our room, or yours, or your sister's. But no, he chose the bathroom.'

'Maybe he felt dirty.'

'Why dirty?'

'I don't know. I've got to go. I've got to be at college.'

'Don't you miss us?'

'No.'

'You're lying. You miss us, don't you?'

'At the weekend. The weekend's when I miss you.'

'I miss you every day. I mean, I miss you both. It's so difficult living without you. I love you both.'

When I was little, we lived in Gonesse, Sarcelles for a bit, and then Paris. And then my father finally became rich (again). My mother decided to stop dying her hair blonde and come to terms with its natural colour, black. He started losing weight when all his friends were putting it on. She got scared that he was becoming anorexic, so she started to re-dye her hair. She became blonde again. He bought her a ring, a big rock from Boucheron, because Boucheron were the only jewellers she liked. One year he didn't want to go away on holiday, he said he'd been everywhere, so they bought a beautiful apartment in Cannes, even though they both hated the Southern heat. He sent his two children to New York to finish their education: up until then, he thought it'd been too French. He said that a Jew has got to be international because everyone expects a Jew to be from nowhere. Gonesse, Sarcelles, Paris, Cannes, New York.

My mother's woken me up at seven o'clock. She knows she's going to wake me up, but it's one o'clock in the afternoon in Paris and she's bored, so she calls.

She tells me about the benefit she organised at the Pavillon Gabriel for an orphans' charity – probably Jewish – the name of which I've forgotten. Le Tout Paris was there but Line Renaud, who apparently is a great Friend of Israel (oh yes?) dropped out at the last minute because she had to go to Las Vegas or some-where. In any case, Israel's ambassador was there, it was the least he could do. Do I understand? Do I need money? Yes, the whole time. Same as usual. Am I taking care of my little sister? Yes. Is she all right, is she getting on OK? She's getting on OK. And your screenplay? It's coming along. Can I tell you a secret? No! Please, she begs.

She wonders, as she does every other conversation, who could possibly be the one in her family, out of her uncles, her grandfathers and her brothers, who was mad on movies. I suggest she look on Papa's side of the family, but she insists on looking on her own. Perhaps, she says from the other side of the Atlantic, perhaps it comes from your grandfather. He always wanted to do photography.

She says she wants to have a face-lift and what do I think. Aunt Adèle knows a very good surgeon, a Tunisian Jew who they say does wonders. Women come from all over the world to this Benamou to have a face-lift . . . or is it Benchétrit . . . No, Benamou. Can you believe it, he charges sixty thousand francs for a nose job. It's outrageous! Oh well, never mind, I'll grow old, she says, but with a six-hour advantage. You've got to go through with it all without cheating, do I agree. I don't know, Mum, I've never been interested when you talk about wrinkles. She replies that I'm not interested in anything, anyway, and perhaps she should just have her nose done. Jews all over the world have had their noses done. Even the goys have started. Haven't you seen them in the street and on TV? They've all got the same nose. I tell her that her nose is fine as it is. It's straight, proud and intriguing. My nose intriguing? She starts laughing at last. I like it when she laughs. My nose intriguing! There, you see, I've absolutely got to have it done because if you're intriguing, that means people ask questions and all I want is not to be noticed. We already draw too much attention to ourselves, us Jews. Got to keep a low profile. Mum! Your nose is fine as it is!

She asks me again if I need money and I give the same answer, that I always need money. You're my son, there's no doubt about that, she replies. She says that she misses me and she wonders why her two children have left her to go and live in New York. I tell her again that it's so we can learn how to breathe, or maybe it's to make her suffer, or maybe it's simply that we're afraid of staying in France and that one day they might just herd us onto trains and I've always felt like being sick on trains. She laughs and asks me if I can really imagine myself being herded onto a TGV. By the time the French get up the courage to throw us out, we'll already be in Israel, or New York, or Hong Kong, at any rate somewhere where life isn't too boring, where there'll be something to do, where she can organise her get-togethers to save the little orphans in Israel.

Your nose is fine the way it is, Mum.

Why don't I ask about Papa, am I angry, and if I'm angry, I shouldn't be because, after all, he's making a great sacrifice to pay for our studies, mine and my sister's, not to mention the flat right in the middle of Manhattan, the clothes, the trips to Paris etc.? Do I realise how hard it is for him? The least I could do is ask about my father who's sweating blood for us.

How's Papa?

She says that since the bathroom episode, he's not the same any more. He's started spending more and more time with rabbis and he's even planning on coming to New York to see the Rabbi. Which Rabbi? I ask her. What do you mean, which Rabbi? she goes on, shocked, as if I'd forgotten to tidy my room. They say he's the next Messiah. They do remarkable work, those people, you know. One of the young ones stopped your father on Avenue Montaigne – can you believe that, they come as far as Avenue

Montaigne – and they made him lay tefillin. It's been thirty years since he's laid tefillin! He agreed to do it and started crying in their van, because, can you believe it, they drive around the whole of Paris in vans. Vans which they've turned into little synagogues. Your father started crying and he told me that he couldn't stop. They told him that it was his soul waking up, because, in the end, the soul of a Jew always wakes up, and that it wasn't worth seeking elsewhere that which he'd find within himself. The long and short of it is that your dear father wants us to eat kosher at home. Kosher! Mind you, they do say kosher meat is better for you. I can't find a butcher anywhere near us. He's even decided to observe the sabbath. Can you imagine your father observing the sabbath! He's started putting time-switches all over the house and he pays the concierge to punch in the digital door-code for him to get into the building, because, in case you'd forgotten, on the sabbath even touching a switch is out of the question. Electricity's like fire, forbidden on Saturdays. I don't know if it's a temporary thing or if the nightmare is only just beginning. Yes, that's right, I said 'nightmare'. I've always been proud to be Jewish but now he's going too far. He asked me to ring the wife of one of the ones he met in the mobile synagogue so that she can teach me to make sabbath bread for Kiddouch on Friday evenings. I said to him, 'Tell me I'm dreaming,' and tears welled in his eyes. Emotional blackmail. So, anyway I agreed to call this woman who I don't know. Do you think he could be going mad?

What about you, Mum, what do you think? Sweetheart,

what do I think, are you really asking me what I think? Since you left, everything in our life has started changing. I think that when you take away a single brick the others had better find their place pretty quickly, otherwise the whole house which has been built up with such patience, collapses. What I think, sweetheart, is that I should be moving as well, like the rest of you. I just have to find a direction. I ask her if that's the reason she wants to get her nose done. Perhaps, she says. Perhaps.

Then she asks me if I remember that song which I used to listen to non-stop when I was a teenager. By David Bowie, that singer who looked like one of her girlfriends. You know, that song called 'Changes'. I found the album in your room and put it on on your stereo at top volume. It reminded me of when you were here. It's sad, that song, don't you think?

Abdourahman Waberi

The Gallery of the Insane

Abdourahman Waberi

Hell is empty and all the devils are here!   Shakespeare

Nobody's to blame.   Evelyn Waugh

Asky so blue that it is almost white. An area of the poor quarter of Djibouti. A wooden house, just like the rest, with an aluminium roof. On the filthy roof riddled with holes, eaten away as much by rust (humidity reigns supreme) as by wear and tear, here and there the most surprising objects are juxtaposed and reverberate with strange echoes: a burst ball shrivelled by the heat, an old battered bicycle wheel, a dilapidated straw hat, a worn-out shoe, a rag, a few wretched nails.

In a shady corner of the verandah, back against the partition, an elderly man is seated on a raffia mat. Before him, a low, rickety table on which are placed side by side a little red ice jug for keeping water cool, a Thermos for tea which is hot and fragrant with spices (cinnamon, cloves, cardamom and ginger), a glass and a cup. Right under the spout of the ice jug, wrapped in cloth kept constantly wet: khat, the most desirable plant in this corner of the world. The magic plant. One that brings misfortune. Khat looks like twigs held together by a cork-coloured strand from a banana leaf.

This man, with the half-closed eyes of someone who has stayed up all night, is my father. Awaleh ruminates, as we say, with great pride. If the truth be told, he does not ruminate, he chews his khat the way you chew tobacco. Or chewing gum for that matter. And every fifteen minutes or so, he drinks a mouthful of cold water, then some hot tea. Khat makes you thirsty. Khat gives you pins and needles in your legs. My father changes position every half hour; after leaning on his right side (the one he prefers), he leans to the left. It is always the same routine. Always. People's lives follow the rhythm of khat in this damned country. Without khat life has no point! From 1 pm to 8 pm, khat keeps men (and women) alive. Without it, what does one do, how does one live? Only the solitary voice of the muezzin manages to disturb, for a few, this deeply ingrained ritual.

In a world set adrift, people cling to the most fragile thing imaginable; the sprigs of an Ethiopian shrub. This plant repays them with an ability to endure. Khat is poison and its antidote, in other words, life imprisonment.

The most deadly fires always occur on afternoons when, in a state of lethargy, men, women, children and animals yearn to get lost in a world of dreams. A few muddy lanes away, a tiny house is being consumed by flames. The firemen oblige everyone to wait as if they were the messiah. Just like always. What does it matter? It is said they no longer know which way to turn. Last week a ninety-year-old mentally ill woman died exhausted, suffocated under the ruins. A handful of ashes seemed to indicate all that remained of her, hours later, when the fire was finally quelled by impassive neighbours.

Abdourahman Waberi

Fire, that malevolent Prometheus, does the job of the town planning people beautifully. Within public view, fire, in a crazy dance, toils at tracing alleyways that zigzag through the poor quarter, sweeping everything in its path like the woeful river Acheron, leaving behind nothing but gnarled, stunted stumps, slate-black in colour.

More recently, in front of some powerless victims, a leading town planning official uttered a dull pronouncement: 'Fire spares no one but we should recognise that we only get the fires we deserve. You may have noticed that we never even lament the damage caused by some pyromaniac in the heart of town.' In our part of town fire is free to act at will.

Hesitant like some tiny craft, life struggles in the hollow belly of a little girl; a girl-child with an emaciated face feeds a child that is just as half-starved. Which is the mother? Which one the offspring?

In the meantime, a small distance away, my father is seated on his raffia mat. Back against the partition as usual, he chews away instinctively. There is a racket outside. The hot wind stiffens people's faces into a mask-like immobility. The roads empty of passers-by, life slows down, liquefies. No longer will there be anyone in the lanes. The hustle and bustle will evaporate. The bewitching hour approaches stealthily. Khat takes its hold over the town. Nothing else counts as zombification sets in. The outside world has ceased to exist. It is the bewitching hour.

In the asphaltless, dusty alleyways where rubbish, marl and

mounds of dung pile up, a few women chatter in their doorways. The one opposite yells: 'Horror of a child, the devil's very offspring, fetch an ice-cold Coca-Cola for your absent father! Don't play deaf, you know very well that khat dries up his throat. Come here you little bastard!'

Her neighbour follows suit in a tremulous voice as if to lend credence to what she says: 'It is the same with my husband. Without Coca-Cola, the khat would come out of his behind like a baby stricken with a bad case of diarrhoea.' This woman, a nurse's assistant in the local dispensary, likes to impress her neighbours by using new terms systematically borrowed from the hospital-world. A third one, tall and black, with breasts flat against her chest which can be easily seen under her transparent wrap, declares in turn: 'Mine is like a child. I have never seen a grown man with such a sweet tooth. Three Coca-Colas and very sweet tea every day. Sometimes, I wonder whether he didn't suck Coca-Cola from the breast of that weird mother of his.'

From a yard round the back comes the monotonous voice of Said Hamarghod, the most prolific singer in the Somali language, repeating the same everlasting refrain:

> . . . *I do not complain*
> *I am born to suffer pain*
> *One day I will get well*
> *One day I will get well . . .*

Abdourahman Waberi

My father chews away in his corner. Acquaintances, cousins, close and distant relatives, tribal connections and sundry associates vie with each other to greet him. Some come to accompany him in his chewing, some to borrow a bundle of khat which will never be paid for. Each finds a small spot on which to place his bony behind. At 2 p.m. everyone is ready. The khat session has begun. It is the bewitching hour.

Hamoud, the blacksmith, is one of the most effaced people of the neighbourhood. Nevertheless, his peers acknowledge his dexterity, unsurpassed especially in the poor quarters. True to his reputation, it is at this suicidal hour, the time when the sun's arrows are sharper than glass from a broken bottle, that Hamoud gets to his place of work: a heap of scrap iron which serves as his open-air workshop. According to local gossip (which often sheds light on the Great History), Hamoud is a Toumal, which means he belongs to a caste considered inferior; therefore scorned and ostracised by the Somali community as a whole. The Toumals, because they work in metal, are victims of a real segregation that is not openly acknowledged. In our neighbourhood, malicious rumour-mongers claim that Hamoud is excessively addicted to the Devil's brew. Others solemnly swear by their great grandfather, dead as a consequence of the Great Drought referred to as 'The Exterminator', that Hamoud conceals his litre of wine in the bottle of syrup for dry coughs which he hides under his iron bed. Among the blacksmith's enemies are quite a few devout worshippers at the mosque, the leading one being the district chief, Haji War Amoussa. Once, in an indescribable fit of anger, War Amoussa almost put out the eye of one of Hamoud's apprentices, an emaciated mechanic-blacksmith to whom you would hesitate to give a precise age. Halloul did not try to make a complaint since he knew for sure that War Amoussa was untouchable. Rumour had it that an old marital dispute partly explained the blinding hatred that War Amoussa had for Hamoud.

At the end of an alleyway pitted with countless puddles, two classmates of unusual maturity converse energetically (as no university exists in this country, you are termed an intellectual once you even set foot in a state school).

The first says to the second: 'Our country is such a monumental hell-hole that Antonin Artaud himself wouldn't have disowned it!'

The second replies in the same solemn tone: 'At Independence and after, we have had nothing, not even an enlightened demagogue to inspire us with never-ending speeches, or tell us about national advancement – in a word to beguile us with illusions, or rather, frustration . . .'

Bob Marley's voice singing 'Waiting in Vain' echoes from another alleyway.

At 3 p.m., the first signs of life – a prelude to Mirghan[*] – were noticeable in the broad daylight. You get up to stretch your

---

[*] Mirghan: the particular twilight time when khat achieves its paroxysmal effect, also referred to as Solomon's time.

legs a bit. While you're at it, you take the opportunity to go to the cesspit, with its swarms of flies, its network of spiders' webs, its countless geckos, its fat purple cockroaches and its huge rats, to empty your bladder. The more alert chewers reluctantly go to the nearby shop to buy a second bottle of Coca-Cola or a third packet of foreign cigarettes. The most insatiable – there were quite a few – forget their pride in order to borrow another bundle of khat to the great distress of their usual supplier, my father for instance. The more restrained ones – they were rare – economise by frugally chewing their meagre sprigs of khat. The latter do not throw away either the leaves that are hard to chew or those that hurt the tongue; those leaves which are usually given to the beggars and madmen who scrounge around the area.

Each district has its horde of madmen. Each madman suffers from his own characteristic form of lunacy, cultivating its particular attributes, managing his type of insanity as only he understands it. Each madman represents a fully-fledged brand of dementia. Some are distinguished by an innate charm and a certain unique allure.

There are the energetic madmen, generally the throwers of stones. Spiteful and bad-tempered, usually they first attack children, women, drunkards – the latter yet another breed of madmen roaming this country – and the sick or those alleged to be so. The energetic madmen fear competition, perceived as insolent and treacherous, from the armies of beggars, many of whom are from the multitude of refugees, bludgeoned into exile or driven away by barbed wire, by different governments. The energetic madmen denounce, to all those willing to listen, the shameless and insulting mendicancy of these rascals from elsewhere, therefore from nowhere. Fiercely jealous of their patch (for they are the real sons of our soil), the energetic madmen hunt down normal people and foreigners. They can be murderous. The true children of our neighbourhood, they have retained memories of distant battles, including those fought for Independence.

'We – us energetic madmen – we were the most ardent of nationalists. We fought the French. We left the most valiant of our number on those fields of glory at Poudrière, Gabode, Loyada and as for the front-lines where the enemy soldiers were more numerous than flies on an open wound . . . To hell with it, all that is the past, gone with the wind . . . You want to know the truth: at present we understand nothing. Honestly, we are saddened by the passing of the time of Khaireh Addeh,* which at least had the advantage of clarity. However, we are not stupid, we know that France has not been the same since Giscard d'Estaing. Since then, everything has been but a great black abyss. Those who rule us have outshone us in the field of insanity, those so-called professionals, in other words energetic madmen . . .'

There are also the malevolent madmen, unmatched sycophants and unsurpassed flatterers. Of them it is said that they

---

* Khaireh Addeh: the name that people from Djibouti jokingly give the French and by extension all whites. Addeh also means light.

are in such a state out of necessity, because they can do nothing else. As their victims they prize women above all else, wealthy or not, to whom they offer advice which must be paid for in full, immediately. For they know how to reach the soft spot in each one of their prey. They content themselves with just one insane scream (once said to be typical of Blacks) when faced by difficult cases.

'Ladies, you are the most beautiful, most generous, most sincere, most noble; we detect this deep within you, we can sense the slightest sign hidden in the mysteries of your personality, come on, pay us in khat today, Friday, the day of our Lord and not of Jesus Christ. The stars could not be more favourable, therefore everything will go well for all of you! It is written in the folds along your necks and on the fleshiest parts of your inside thighs.'

This delighted more than one maiden awaiting a well-arranged marriage.

In contrast to the malevolent madmen is the band of silent madmen. Their distinguishing feature: a luxuriant head of hair just like the devotees of Saint Haile Selassie of Harar and Saint Tafari of Jamaica. Formerly renowned for their wisdom and as holy men, the direct descendants of the priests of the Horn of Africa, it is rumoured that they have been afflicted since then by a kind of pernicious grace. The silent madmen enjoy the luxury of not breathing a word, all the while scratching their heads and backs as if, without the whole world realising, they are carefully keeping intact the secrets that control the universe. They have a look that cuts through you, that penetrates you, which makes fools believe that these men must possess something of the mystical. Speechless as Buddhas, their silence can make your blood run cold. People attribute to them glorious pasts or amorous adventures which are out of the ordinary.

'You know why this man is silent?' says a normal man pointing to a silent madman.

'Apparently on his wedding day, his ninth wife died of suffocation, like the eight others before her,' he adds.

In any case, one thing is certain: the silent madmen make others speak. And consequently bring them alive.

There are not only madmen, but also madwomen in this part of the world, where genuine press reporting lost out to rumour some time ago. Among the hordes of madwomen are the sexual exhibitionists. They provoke an outcry whenever they troop by. Their high rank ensures that they are followed by a pack of small boys, many of whom are being trained for the profession of itinerant madman, wildly encouraged by the authorities at a loss for what to do. Thus, the sexual exhibitionists, like veritable queen bees, never travel about without their swarms of drones. At peak hours, at each crossroads, a sexual exhibitionist skilfully lifts her wrap in order to show off her trump card. She is especially successful when facing the devout congregation at the mosque. The faithful no longer pretend to avert their eyes from these representatives of Lucifer, but enjoy themselves when confronted by such a confused show of withered genitalia and shrivelled lips stinking of faeces, urine and the foam left by men in a hurry so as not to be caught with a notorious, infamous sexual exhibitionist. In fact, these madwomen make many happy but are rewarded only with harsh words (like the government, they are taken for granted by the nation).

'We are goddesses, you call on us often, come on, when will we have a temple of our own?' demands one.

Ultimately, there are the madmen who bear their insanity with noble grace. The masters of Somalian alliterative or elliptical poetry, these are the highest-ranking of the profession and also the most feared. These men are dangerous. These are the mad-men who reason, the tellers of truth, the summoners of heavenly thunderbolts. They are becoming increasingly scarce. Their kind is heading for extinction. They throw mimosa spines at the enemy in question: distinguished persons of whatever kind, for instance. They challenge with bravura and bravery the most respected figures in the nation, in other words the Prophet and the President of the Republic. When a madman who speaks truths goes any-where, everyone falls silent: some make a hasty exit on tiptoe, others break into a heavy sweat – for no particular reason – others claim to want to vomit, to have pins and needles in their legs or to have difficulty holding back their urine. The most brazen, like Haji War Amoussa, try to corrupt these madmen: 'Here is the Devil incarnate, give him a drink! Are you thirsty? Look, take this bundle of khat and this note to pay for your bus fare to that rotten slum Balbala Soub'han'Allah, go on, go, my son . . .'

And the reasoning madman gives as good as he gets. He delves deep into the chief's past to unearth repressed secrets, camouflaged events, false identities or taboo incidents: 'Tell me Haji, whence this display of generosity from you – you who recently fought with vultures over offal and entrails in order to sell the spoils at the highest price in the market? And your twelfth pilgrimage, how was it paid for? In the most dishonest way possible, I presume?'

The madman who speaks truths is terrible when he opens his mouth. He is fond of using shocking turns of phrase and has achieved a level of fluency and insight justly appreciated and recognised by all. Some see in him the moral conscience – if there is one – of the neighbourhood. This lunatic knows the individual value of each person in a mass society which suffocates the individual. He rewards the virtuous – harder and harder to find – and punishes in his own way the spiteful, the arrogant, the oppressive, the disloyal, thieves, tricksters, upstarts and, last but not least, those with tribal prejudices. That is why his enemies are more numerous than prayer beads on a chaplet. They always demand that an example be made of him, they repeat everywhere that he should be drawn and quartered for the enormity of his insolence, for his failure to respect tradition. But the madman who speaks many truths persists in tracking down hypocritical bigots and exposing in the public square their peculiar vices: this one is a homosexual, the other an inveterate drinker, and so on.

The madman who demystifies vehemently attacks opportunists of every description. And with an urgent immediacy, the all-seeing visionary madman fighting against the 'topsy-turvy world' pronounces his personal code of conduct: 'I have nothing against the suffering of humanity, I, the clairvoyant madman! I eliminate the bad seed. Ah! Ah! Ah! Be warned: I am a thousand years old . . .'

Leaning against the partition, my father continues to chew.

Mounsi

Into the Void

In the middle of the capital's ring-road, surrounded by the rumble of metal, between the lanes, in the rush of cars, motorbikes, buses, the smell of petrol and the deafening din of the city, a man prays. He has spread a white sheet before his face and neither the curses nor the jeers of the drivers stop him from his slow ritual of prostration. He prays on the tarmac as if on Holy Ground. Slowly, he inclines the coppery mask of his face. There, in the middle of the ring-road, he heard the muezzin's call to evening prayer, a voice borne by the wind like a wail for his heart to hear. He senses around him the breath of silence. It is as if the world had stopped moving and speaking. As if the cars had been transformed into stones. He breathes deeply, his mouth on the ground, listening to the blood throbbing in his throat, in his ears. His cheekbones protrude from a black-bearded face; an old cap is perched at an angle on his head; his eyes are glazed over. His shirt and trousers hang from him pitifully. His hands are sticky with a blackish grease. He throws back his head and begins to pray. He leans forward in the opposite direction, towards the palms of his hands. He stays bent over like this for a while. He gazes elsewhere, beyond the world of men and the walls of the city. His eyes stare, far away, at the ceiling of the sky where lies infinity. In the light of the sun, he sees white cities, springs, caravans of camels and donkeys laden with goods. In the middle of the ring-road floats the mirage of a minaret. In his eyes: hunger, thirst, fatigue, madness. He prays on the tarmac as if on Holy Ground.

On a sand-strewn course, following the blackened bed of dried-up torrents, he walks under a sky blazing with light. He inhales the breath of the wind. He goes down to a spring where he bathes his face between his hands, kneeling on the soil, like one returning from a long journey. And so he remains on the cracked, hardened, baked earth. The sun at its zenith burns like a flame. He is over there, in the midst of chants, of locusts and wasps, among shepherds, flocks of goats and sheep, and thorn bushes. Over there, amid the echoing, clear voices of women, their long fingers stained with henna, singing softly, cradling in their arms fragile infants; chasing away with slow gestures the wispy flies that dance and hum over their heads. He recognises the parchment-dry faces of the old men and women leaning on walls of mud and dry stones. He remembers their first names.

He forgets the concrete walls between which I would wait for him, standing, as if, each time there was a bang, the door would open to reveal the light of his smile, a ray of sunlight between the bars.

Dumped in the kitchen, hidden under the bed, were his bottles of plonk. Any sense of shame completely consumed, like some poisonous wine, so much so that fountains gushing with pure water would seem bitter to his thirst. I could still see him drinking from the bottle. Where else could he have filled and emptied himself of so much at the same time. Gradually, he spoke to no one. Not even to me. He made noises, intestinal growls. That's all.

In the traffic's din, four men in white coats alighted from a vehicle marked with a red cross. They lifted him up by the hands and legs. They swept him into the air. He ended up with his arms in a cross, on the hood of the ambulance. Spread-eagled, he groaned softly, closing his eyes.

'He's dead drunk,' the drivers said.

'I saw God!' screamed the man.

The four nurses wearing the uniform of the local state hospital slipped a straitjacket on him. He was whisked away in a wail of sirens. The following morning I was woken by knocking on the door. The doorbell was broken. I got up to let them in, half dressed. Everyone was there. There was a veritable throng in the room. First of all, the neighbour and the social worker, then the caretaker accompanied by men from the Department of Health. The place had a musty smell, a stench of wine and a faint odour of tobacco.

'Incredible ... got to like filth to live in this dump,' the caretaker kept on saying as she opened every cupboard.

Someone remembered it was wrong to talk like that in front of a 'kid'.

'Well! Don't you think I'm saying this for his benefit?'

The man from the council responsible for our tower block put his hand on my shoulder, in a friendly gesture, and assured me, as he rubbed my head affectionately, that he had called for help from the social services so that I would be in need of nothing.

'It's for your own good,' he added.

I didn't care. I wasn't even listening to them. I couldn't even cry. I felt like a dried-up fountain. For years, he had worked in one of those factories where a grease-laden belt clanked above the workers' heads. Following the rhythm of the machine, the men's fingers fitted metal parts. That's where he worked twelve hours a day, between the double row of machine tools where each worker was busy at his bench, in tandem with two teams, each one with its movements carefully calculated, sequenced beforehand.

At the day's end he would come home. Drained. Each morning he set off again. One day the factory closed. He was fired. But the belt continued to grind away in his tired brain. I feel that a part of him had got caught in the creaking turns of the wheel. He drifted gradually into a state of half-sleep. Walking through the streets, he uttered out loud prayers in Arabic that I didn't understand. His hands counted off old prayer beads. Absent-mindedly, as if he was already dead.

I don't think my father was really mad. He was simply scared of his shadow. Times were hard. Bailiffs, foreclosures, due dates, threats of eviction for non-payment of rent. When they came, I would hear them – those men enforcing the law; those bureaucrats working for the council – laughing at my father's accent in muffled tones.

'You got your money for drink all right, eh, Mustapha . . .'

Mounsi

The entire fate of mankind and of the world lay there, in that wickedness which is everywhere. Ever since people have suffered. They would have known if there was even a little love, here, there, on earth or in heaven.

With his pitiful blind man's shuffle, he would slowly make his way back from bar counters, his head lolling. He walked the narrow streets of the city later and later at night. Heads appearing at windows would point to him and laugh. I heard his heavy footfall echo in the stairwell. More than once he stumbled against a step or injured his head on a wall in the corridor. His head pressed against the door, he would try to fit the tip of his key into the keyhole. Unable to locate the light switch, he didn't care if he got burnt by a match, blackening his skin as it went out. I would get up to let him in. He was asleep on his feet. I smelled on his drunken body the stench of cheap wine. At home I would sometimes hide the bottles. He sought them out as someone dying of thirst would a bubbling spring.

In my eye's unswerving gaze, I hold on to the saddest early memory of them all, that which I discerned in his illiterate eyes, as he made his way to his damnation, shuffling unsteadily, incapable of perceiving those around him. He fell into a strange sleep disturbed by trances, flashes of delirium, sudden jerks. Lying in the same bed, I protected him in my arms against the rats, the snakes and all those creatures which slept at the head of his bed. I was haunted by his face. I watched him sleep as he might do one day, for ever, eyelids closed once and for all.

Feverish, eyes staring, he would awaken, his throat dry, dripping with sweat, lips trembling. He caught back his breath, stopped gasping. As I switched on the light, I showed him the animals which darted for cover, crawling across the floor. Pacified, he smiled at me by way of an excuse for having woken me up in the middle of the night. I knew that at the next bout of drinking, as soon as he had nodded off, the rats lurking in holes in the wall would return to make his teeth chatter with horror. He trembled. I waited for dawn. The bustle of life began outside in absolute indifference. Those who have experienced nights like these no longer have any liking for sleep. He was so harmless, so vulnerable. Later, with all the paltry ferocity I could muster, I avenged him with love, and a hatred of the world, aimed at everything that crossed my path: man, woman, animal. And I am completely unrepentant about the things I did. No one is innocent. No one. Not them, nor I, nor you. I have long felt the desire to disfigure, to defile every living creature by branding them with the stamp of my life. It is fascinating, the suffering of others, their ability to express terror. Those screams, like a cry outside of oneself, uttered by someone else, but in which you hear your own voice. Curiously, later, as I went my way, I would often come across street people with shabby clothes, dishevelled hair and the crazed look of a prophet. Those men who stumble along the pavement. As I passed close by them, they grabbed hold of my sleeve and stared at length into my eyes, motionless.

In their gaze I saw my father's eyes. Alarmed, I beat a hasty retreat.

In our abandoned home, I set about picking up pieces of broken bottles scattered on the floor, with the silent solemnity of a child gathering autumn flowers.

There remained nothing of my father except what memory offered me, until I forgot everything. From child-care centres, to families, to foster homes.

On days mild like sweet cherubim, my legs wide open, knees slightly bent, back arched, when I pissed through the air towards the sky, perhaps I was already pissing in God's direction. Little by little, I learnt no longer to fear anything. I was content to let things take their course and await the inevitable outcome. During the day, I would never tire of looking at the sky. And at night, at the dormitory ceilings. I pressed my fingers with all my might against my eyes, in order to see the stars. When dawn came, my eyelids were black and blue. I wondered if this was so when you died.

As for my father, I saw him only once again, by chance, in the street. But I made sure I did not cross his path. Although his hair had gone white and his back was hunched, I recognised him by that brown-eyed gaze, intensified by his emaciated body.

Mathieu Lindon

F. N. Rally

Tuesday morning. The press coverage focuses on the huge success of the march honouring Julien Thoris and Hadi Benfartouk, and on the evening's incidents. The extreme right had never seemed so active in France as in these last years. There were a few other notable news items. First, the planned rally with Jean-Marie Le Pen at the Place de la Bastille. Though the Paris police prefecture was worried about possible incidents, it finally authorised the event out of fear that banning it would lead to worse. This way, at least the Front National and its security forces would be directly responsible in case of trouble. Second, the apparent change in approach taken by attorney Pierre Mine, the lawyer defending Ronald Blistier, for which the journalists all seemed to take credit. And finally, the lack of progress in the investigation into Julien Thoris's death. This left the Front National leaders free to air any theory that suited their conjectures. Despite witnesses' testimony to the contrary, they claimed it was a settling of scores between rival gangs, none of which had a single white member. The skins and F.N. militants who were questioned about the murder 'had to be released', as several journalists regretfully reported.

The Le Pen rally took place at six-thirty in the evening. Several thousand people milled about in front of a stage erected on the Place de la Bastille. (The police said 2,000, the organisers claimed 20,000. The media reported between 3,000 and 5,000.) This was nothing like the million-odd marchers the previous evening, but it was still significant.

Louis Degrapin, the activist wounded near Saint-Michel at the same time Julien Thoris was being thrown into the Seine a few hundred yards away, was introduced. He had been discharged from hospital only a few hours after being admitted – the doctors quickly decided that the young man's injuries weren't life-threatening – but he appeared on stage swathed in bandages. He'd been able to see the thugs who had brutally attacked him, Degrapin claimed. They were completely berserk, and he had been terrified. He thought he wouldn't get away alive, he said, and was saved only by the last-minute arrival of the CRS riot police. He was surprised that the cops hadn't been able to arrest even one of his attackers, who were 'very recognisable, very typical', as he put it. 'What frightened me the most was that I felt I wasn't even in France. They were fighting me five to one, and we don't do that where I come from.' Shouts of indignation rose from the audience.

The audience was well warmed up when Jean-Marie Le Pen took the stage at seven o'clock. The Bastille Métro station had been closed and the police were keeping counter-demonstrators away from the square. This led to a few skirmishes, which could be heard on the stage and by the audience. Reporters and radio and TV crews had to endure the F.N. militants' hostility. In addition to being yelled at, cameramen wiped spittle off their lenses, and a few reporters had to clean it off themselves. But the journalists hadn't considered boycotting the demonstration, so they stayed where they were, doing their job, pointing their microphones and cameras at Jean-Marie Le Pen.

The focus of all eyes, Le Pen was triumphant, feeding on the hatred he often generates, both loved and loathed, the central personality in a drama that enrages his enemies.

Le Pen's followers cheered him for a long time before he began to address them. He clasped his hands above his head, shouting, 'Thank you, thank you' over the roar of the crowd.

A few excerpts from his oration: 'My friends, thank you for being here with me to affirm that every time someone strikes at us, we will strike back. If people think that we'll just take it, that we'll let ourselves be trampled on and insulted without reacting, we'll prove they're sadly mistaken. It isn't enough to gang up five to one on our supporters, then go and whimper in front of the television cameras – which have always been sympathetic to anyone who attacks the Front National. It isn't enough to threaten the movement I have the honour to lead, or threaten France's millennial renaissance.

'We know who these people are, the ones who shed crocodile tears over the corpse of every Arab and every Black and then parade their feigned suffering in public. If they had to pay one franc in royalties to the family of these victims for every tear they shed, you can be sure their eyes would be a lot drier. In the old days, we used to speak of armchair activists. Today, I suppose we have to talk about ghetto activists, or maybe even cemetery activists.

'You and I know that the people who weep on those occasions aren't weeping in vain. They are writers without readers, intellectuals without ideas, politicians without voters. And they're weeping for their own interests while pretending to pay their respects to these so-called victims. They're looking for customers, and don't care how they get them. But let one Front National supporter be left for dead on the Place de la Bastille after a million anti-racists have held a supposedly 'non-violent' march, and not one of those good souls will show the slightest sign of indignation. After all, maybe our friend hurt himself. Maybe his shoelaces were untied, and he tripped and fell – straight into a coma. This is no joke. I'm telling you, and I'm telling all the anti-nationalists: we won't be the lambs in their sacrifices.

'We're accused of being racists because we defend Frenchmen. That's revealing, isn't it? What brought all those people together, all those demonstrators marching towards the heart of Paris from every outlying suburb in their raggle-taggle procession? What unites them, besides a hatred of Frenchmen and a desire to dilute the centuries of our heritage with their blood?

'You see all these so-called egalitarian anti-racists draw the line at anti-French racism. That's the current fashion. Nobody in Saint-Germain-des-Prés gets upset when whites born in France of French parents have to go to the end of the line to receive family benefits or welfare payments. For that matter, I understand why the welfare people are grateful to those foreigners: they're bureaucrats who would be out of a job if all those people were sent back home, along with all the attendant humanism that Régis Debray and Lionel Jospin wear on their sleeves. As for us, we aren't monsters, we're just Frenchmen who are proud to be French, proud of our fathers and of our fatherland. There are still some of us left. We're said to be an endangered species, but we don't need Madame Voynet's support to reverse the trend. There are still Frenchmen in France, and that isn't good news to everybody. *La France au Français!*

Commentators noted the forcefulness of Le Pen's speech, no doubt largely due to his internal power-struggle with Bruno Mégret, who wants the Front National to acquire a more respectable image. But the thousands of supporters in front of the stage turned Le Pen's appearance into a triumph. They laughed at what he called his jokes, instantly picked up on the slightest nuance, sometimes interrupted him with applause that nobody could claim wasn't spontaneous.

Fired up by its ringleader, the crowd gathered on the Place de la Bastille consisted mainly of energetic young men itching for a fight. If you'd searched them, you'd have found concealed weapons by the hundreds. They would have liked nothing better than for left-wing groups to decide on a strategy of confrontation. In many ways, the atmosphere was pre-insurrectionary. But the mood in the democrats' camp, as the journalists present noted, was more one of disgust than of panic. The leftists weren't so much afraid of an immediate fascist coup d'état as of a kind of gangrene – a social disease that might be temporarily stopped or driven back, but never quite cured. There seemed to be no way of stamping it out. It was as if Jean-Marie Le Pen put all of society on the defensive.

As the rally broke up, clashes seemed inevitable. The police presence, like the media's, was enormous. LCI, the TV news channel, was broadcasting live continuously from La Bastille, give or take a few commercial breaks. But the reporters were eventually forced to pack up their microphones, because nothing was happening.

During Le Pen's speech, so as not to be constantly filming the leader, the crews occasionally turned their cameras on the audience, focusing on some of his listeners. Most were young men with close-cropped hair, the core of the Front National. The 'respectable' bourgeoisie stayed home, preferring to turn out for the 14 July celebrations. As demos go, this one was gripping. Nice clothes risked getting ripped; nice people risked physical violence. This was the Front National proletariat, to whom the party offered the possibility of meteoric ascents. An outsider might have seen the rally as a gang of marauders ready for pillage, awaiting only the enemy's retreat to cut loose. It was as if they had laid siege to society, but the moment of surrender was forever being delayed. These were the Front National's warriors, not its ideologues, and they were restless, eager for physical combat.

LCI also broadcast a few interviews with F.N. sympathisers, designed to help viewers understand what made them tick, and ran them in a short live report.

'I'm a fan of Le Pen's because he understands everything,' said a brutish-looking youth. 'He agrees with us. He's for equality. There's no reason everything should go to the rich and the immigrants. We should just fight one on one, and then you'll see who's strongest.'

'I'm for the republic,' said another, 'and so was my grandfather, who died for France in Algeria. But I don't understand why it would be any less a republic if France were made up just of Frenchmen. It's called the French Republic, right? You want to live here, you've got to be republican and French, that isn't so hard to understand, is it?'

Said a third, a follower of Bruno Mégret: 'What's the use of talking to the media, so everything we say can be used against us? What business is it of yours if I vote Front National, so long as I vote Front National and there are more and more of us? We vote for the Front National because we feel like it. If you don't like it, so much the better.'

A fourth, to a reporter whose outstretched microphone never wavered: 'I vote Front National because I don't have the right to beat the shit out of you. But if you want, I'll beat the shit out of you, with pleasure.'

A fifth: 'I'll come right out and say what everybody is thinking: if Raymond Blistier didn't kill that Arab kid, then it's a shame that he's in prison. And if he did kill him, it's still a shame.'

His mate, leaning towards the camera: 'If he didn't kill him, go ahead and throw Blistier in jail. But what if he did kill him? What did you want him to do, kiss him on the mouth?'

And the two went off, laughing loudly.

'The risks of live TV . . .' said the LCI presenter, for fear that the network would be accused of the racism that was being so crudely expressed.

Mathieu Kassovitz

La haine

33
A Street ... Ext. Day

Young guys scatter down a street. At the other end, far away, Abdel's brother's car is visible, it has pulled up by Samir. Insults are heard and suddenly the barrel of a rifle sticks out of the car window.

BROTHER ABDEL – Ehhh, the filth!

The blast reverberates through the council estate. One of the car passengers has just shot Samir. He hits the ground.

The young guys pause to see the car speed off with a screeching of tyres, but 100 metres on a police van blocks its route and it tries to swerve, sadly only to wind up hitting a wall.

From a distance, the young guys see the car passengers getting nicked. A violent arrest; dangerous. The police haul out the marksmen and throw them on the ground. Samir's wounded in the arm.

It's serious, and the watchers hurry towards the police van into which the car passengers are already being loaded.

More than thirty young guys materialise by the van to take on the police, Vinz and Saïd are among them. Despite his wound, Samir tries to dodge between bodies, helped by Hubert, but he rapidly loses consciousness. The police retrieve Samir after punching him a couple of times, retreat into the van and split, leaving the young guys on the spot.

On the other side of the street is the sound of a battalion of CRS riot police running up fast.

The young guys escape into the council estate.

Some of them, including our three 'heroes', dive into a tower block.

34
Basement passage. Int. Day

Saïd, Vinz and Hubert leg it down the sombre hallway of the tower block, the other young guys behind them splitting up, followed by the sound of the CRS riot police pouring down the stairwell screaming orders as they go. The gang continues its race through the labyrinth, pursued by the CRS who can be heard rushing all over the place.

The gang forks right but Saïd grabs Hubert and Vinz to pull them left. Saïd speeds ahead and turns a corner, not realising that a CRS has just burst out of a side passage, blocking Hubert and Vinz.

Instinctively, Vinz whips out his gun and aims it at the CRS, who freezes.

Hubert, between the two men, takes advantage of their brief stillness to cut short Vinz's intentions. He pushes Vinz, the CRS advances, Hubert thumps him hard and the CRS falls to the ground. Giving him no chance to get up, Hubert stuns him.

Vinz looks on not knowing how to react.

Hubert drags Vinz down one passageway, then another. Saïd is in front of a trapdoor which leads outside.

SAÏD – What the fuck've you done?

They run.

35
Station . . . Ext. Day

The three guys head towards the station leaving the council estate behind them.

Rioters can be heard in the distance.

The platform for Paris is indicated on a station noticeboard.

The three friends run to catch the train coming into the station.

36
Local Fast Train ... Int. Day

Hubert is sitting in a half-full compartment. He looks out of the window to calm himself down, but is extremely agitated. He tries to control his breathing to bring his heartbeat back to normal.

Vinz and Saïd are behind him. The camera stays focused on Hubert who does not respond to Vinz's description of the fight (he's also still charged up with adrenalin).

VINZ (*muttering, finding it hard to control his excitement in front of the other passengers*) – I had the pig at the end of my gun, I swear it, as I see you now. Bastard. Didn't move, shat in his pants I bet ... If Hubert hadn't been there I'd've smoked him, no problem. You should've seen it. Hubert did him over, the pig can't've believed it, two nutters, the likes of which he's never seen before (*he leans towards Hubert*). You went for him, you did it, big time.

Lost in thought, Hubert doesn't answer and looks out at the view, or rather the tower blocks flying past, now and again graffiti bringing a splash of colour to the place though generally it is sad and grey. An old man waits under a trashed, tagged bus shelter, a luxury car rests on breeze-blocks in a wasteland, relieved of its wheels. Further on is the poster featuring the World glimpsed at the beginning of the film. Now you see it clearly – a publicity hoarding for a company with a slogan under the Globe:

THE WORLD IS YOURS

37
Paris ... Ext. Day

The trio is on a vast esplanade.
Paris spreads out in front of them.
It's a whole other vibe, a whole other world. The problems of
the council estate don't exist here.
The sound of the city fills the void.
The atmosphere is totally different, as much at the level of
sound as of vision.
Everything becomes much, much more aggressive.

38
Paris Square ... Ext. Day

The three guys are sitting on a bench in the middle of a very
noisy square. Bored shitless.
Long silence and then . . .

VINZ – So, now what?

SAÏD – Dunno about you, but me, I need to get my dosh
back

Saïd gets up and goes towards a phone booth. He kicks it.

SAÏD *(to the two others)* – How can you make a call if you
haven't got a fiver to blow on a phonecard?

39
Toilets, Bar ... Int. Day

The trio are in the toilets of a bar.
Saïd, Rio Crush in hand, is on the phone, while behind him,
Vinz is taking a welcome piss in the latrines.
Hubert is washing his face in front of the mirror.
Saïd is trying to get information, to track down Asterix's
address.

SAÏD *(aside, to the two others)* – At a quid fifty a Rio Crush
I need to get my dollars tonight

The others don't react. There's tension between them. Hubert
looks at himself for a while in the mirror. Saïd returns to the
phone, asks for some information, and has to wait again. Saïd
turns to the others.

SAÏD – That's enough, how long are you gonna be pissed
at each other?

VINZ – Who's fucking pissed off? Me, I'm not pissed off.
Look at him

SAÏD – You're so boring, I can't believe it. You're like two
kids

HUBERT – Who's a kid?

SAÏD – I said you're both kids. Dissing each other over
bullshit

HUBERT – Wanting to kill a cop, that's really stupid

VINZ *(to Saïd)* – Tell your mate to leave it out OK? I never
said I was going to kill a cop

SAÏD – Yes, you said it

VINZ – That's not what I said

SAÏD – Yes it is

VINZ – I said that *if* Abdel dies I'd do a cop, I didn't say I'd knock off a cop for a laugh. But the other CRS, that one, if I hadn't had a gun we'd've been slaughtered. I'm not Malik Oussekine, I'm not gonna get beaten to death in a basement

HUBERT – Big difference. You're right mate . . . anyway you're always right. And you think we'd spend our Sundays bringing you oranges behind bars?

VINZ – I don't rely on anybody and definitely not on a guy who sells his soul to the enemy

Hubert sighs in despair. Saïd is having a laugh.

VINZ *(very concerned, very stubborn)* – You can laugh, but me, I've had enough of being fucked up the arse by the system every day, we live like dogs in kennels up there, and you're doing fuck all about it. Listen to me, I'm telling you because you're my friends: if Abdel dies, me, I'm going to get even. A cop will die so they see we won't turn the other cheek . . .

SAÏD – Seriously, you sound like a cross between Moses and Bernard Tapie

HUBERT – Who d'you think you're fighting? You think you'll get even? You're mad. Sad fucker. It's guys like you with your Tesco-Rapper mentality are screwing up the estates. If you'd gone to school instead of pissing about with graffiti you'd know there's one thing history taught us: hate attracts hate

VINZ – Are you teaching me lessons in morality now? You're so superior are you, you can just tell us what is good and right and what isn't? Why don't you ever see it my way? Why are you always on the side of those motherfuckers?! Me, I live in the street, and if there's one thing the street taught me, it's that turn the other cheek and you're screwed.

HUBERT – What are you talking about? Fucking arsehole?! You've just held up a cop with a copper's gun, you could've got us killed!!!

The sound of water flushing cuts short Hubert's flow. The three guys turn towards the toilets which are in the same area as they are, they hadn't noticed the little man now coming out of the bog who goes to wash his hands, making his way between Hubert and Vinz who are silent and uncomfortable. The little man washes his hands and looks at the others in the mirror.

THE MAN – It does the world of good to have a good shit

The three guys look at each other, amazed.

THE MAN – Do you believe in God?

The three guys' glances fuse and they respond in gibberish.

THE MAN – At any rate, the thing is not to ask if you believe in God but if God believes in us . . . Me, I think he believes in us, since God helps us and pushes out the crap, you know that?

The three guys smile without answering.

THE MAN – When I was young I had a friend called Grunwalski. We were deported together to Dachau and then, when we got out, to Siberia. When you go to the work camps in Siberia you're transported in cattle trains which cross the frozen steppes, not passing anyone for whole days at a time. We kept warm together, but the problem was that to relieve oneself, to have a shit in the carriage wasn't possible, and the only times we stopped was to refill the engine with water. But Grunwalski was very prudish, even at Dachau, he got embarrassed when we had to wash together. And me, I often teased him about it. So, the train stops and everyone grabs the chance to take a shit behind the carriages. I'd given Grun such a hard time he preferred to go a little further away. And when the train sets off, everyone leaps back on because the train won't wait. Problem is that Grunwalski who'd gone behind a bush hadn't finished shitting. (The old man begins to smile as the images come back to him.) So I see him appear from behind the bush holding up his trousers with both hands to stop them from falling down and he tries to catch up with the train. I hold out my hand, but each time he holds out his, he lets go of his trousers, which fall round his ankles. He hoists up his trousers and runs on, and each time he reaches out to me his trousers fall down

The three guys look at the old man and smile at his story.

SAÏD – So, what happened?

THE MAN – Nothing. Grunwalski froze to death

The trio's smiles fade instantly. As for the old man, he continues to reminisce about his friend, smiling, and then he takes his leave. The trio look at each other uncomfortably.

SAÏD – Why'd he tell us that story?

The others don't answer.

SAÏD – Ehh, why'd he tell us that story?

Christov Rühn a.k.a. DJ Tov

Lost in Music

Christov Rühn a.k.a. DJ Tov

to Miriam and my son, Martin Luther

'What is essential is invisible to the eye; it is only with the heart that one can see rightly' Antoine de Saint-Exupéry, *The Little Prince*

Paris. The end of the '80s is in sight. In the underground scene we hear talk about a new movement from Ibiza which is revolutionising the UK. Acid House. I'm tired of playing in rock groups. It bores me. I've a raging desire to record an Acid track, I need a fix. I love the new and the dangerous. In the 18ème I unearth a young singer. He's called Darling Mayo. Frenchy but chic.

London. Pierre, a TV-producer friend of mine, calls me just as I'm about to leave for London to mix Darling Mayo's track. He wants to know if I'd take part in a documentary about 'the most important musical phenomenon since the advent of punk in the UK' which he's filming for Spanish TV. A few lines and a bottle of champagne later, I say yes.

Acid House. When we land in Camden armed with mikes and cameras, we're amazed by the attitude of these English kids in their 'smiley' T-shirts. An incredible scene flashes before us. In the smallest of shops, on every street-corner, tranced-out kids are dancing, eyes dilated, smiles fixed on faces streaming with sweat. This music is from elsewhere. Electronic music with a mental percussion rhythm, it's a mixture of Kraftwerk and Black

American funk. D-Mob's track 'Aciiid' pumps up the tempo. And it's only five in the afternoon. Check this out. I feel my life has changed. The world is about to change. We've just stepped into the twenty-first century.

Party. My mate Simon, singer, poser and avant-garde artist, invites us to go with him to 'Spectrum' that night at the club Heaven. You don't say no to paradise. Planted at the entrance, a bouncer informs us firmly that no way can we film inside the club. Fact is, the place belongs to Richard Branson, and the week before, the BBC filmed a scandalous yet spectacular programme along the lines of 'our kids are taking drugs as they dance to barbaric music'. XTC. All the organisers are under police surveillance. Too bad. So we head off to another party: Jenny and Danny Rampling's 'Shoom'. Walking on the moon. My first pill. Bingo! I dance as though there's no tomorrow. Savagely sexy. Violently happy.

Paris. As soon as I get back to the capital I burn with one desire: share this new and fantastic trip, but this time with my mates. I've just had proof that the sun shines harder in the hearts of those who turn towards the light – in those whose body and soul get lost in music. My first party happens in les Caves du Chapelais, Place Clichy. This place will become mythical. We decorate it, transform it into a forbidden planet and pump up the volume. I DJ for the first time. I'll never forget it. Impossible, at this precise moment, to realise that this is just the beginning of a period which will take up ten years of my life, of all of our

Christov Rühn a.k.a. DJ Tov

lives: full of joy and happiness, highs and lows, impossible dreams and, most of all, incredible vinyl, vinyl, vinyl. Wonder-full. The soirée is called 'Funky People' and I bring over from London my DJ friends – Eren, who makes a killing mixing one of Disco diva Candy Staton's acapellas with Jamie Principle's and Frankie Knuckles' 'Your Love', and also Charlie Hall, the future founder of the Drum Club. I mix my first records with all the thrill of the first time. The tension goes up, and the most magic moment of all comes straight from space and Larry Heard's classic piece 'Can You Feel It' – the most moving of all tracks in the history of House, and the one which brought us together in that communion of infinite love which so marked this period. Bass junkies and smoke-machine desperadoes: get up, rise up, we're going to church! The vibe is loud. You're inside a dream.

For years, le Tout Paris thinks I'm British. This amuses me since I love to scramble my trails. I'm applying the theories of Guy Debord, the May '68 Situationist, whose philosophy I integrated long ago. Stay free: do not get caught. Under the stones: the beach. We are a nation: the House Nation. Living free is changing the artist's name on each record; destroying the system of production and promotion; profit and share the music. Gimme a melody.

Back then in Paris-Paname, there were just a few of us mad ones putting on such parties. There's Pat Ca$h, the capital's no. 1 bad boy, who creates warehouse parties in derelict tunnels under La Défense (someone told me he's become a rabbi), the club 'Jungle' held every Friday at Le Rex, and Laurent Garnier. He's just got back from the Hacienda in Manchester, where he's resident, in order to fulfil his military service. Every Thursday at Le Palace, on the rue du Faubourg Montmartre, he ignites that legendary English club night, 'Pyramid'.

Laurent is a favourite on the gay scene which absolutely loves his music and is the first to celebrate the new sound. He plays at La Luna, a hardcore gay club in the backstreets of la Bastille, rue Keller. It's the first time girls are allowed in. At no. 1 of that same street, BPM opens, one of my dearly-loved record shops, a temple to House. Founded by Saul, an American who got stuck in Paris, BPM supplies vinyl to all the young Parisian DJs and sells tickets to the raves of the capital. But the mythical club of that period, Boy, is the place where everything is possible. A gay club in the Opéra quarter, under l'Olympia, it would have a major influence on Parisian youth culture, establishing the New Beat Belge, the forerunner of Hard Techno, just before it got closed down. Fazed by the music, boys french-kiss openly on banquettes and girls wander around half naked. The place is thick with sex. The owner of Boy went on to open Le Queen in the '90s, the only big club of the capital. *'14 July 1996, 8am: As those sensible young recruits get ready for the National Parade, a group of drag queens, high and happy, on their way out of Le Queen, go to kiss our valiant soldiers, and smother them in lipstick.'* Order comes from Chaos. God bless Paris.

So, we love each other laced with hits of rainbow-coloured

pills. Paris is burning. It's serious. The trendiest magazine of the '80s, *Actuel*, picks up on Acid House big time, thanks to Ariel Wizman, the Parisian dandy, radio DJ and journalist. Later, Ariel becomes successful with one of the funniest and most subversive talk shows of the '90s, 'La Grosse Boule', on Radio Nova.

They're writing about us. Despite the buzz, Jean-Paul Baudecroux's Radio NRJ, wanting to take control of this movement purely for commercial gain, abandons it fast, following bad press linking House and drugs. In the underground scene we stick together. We cause a sensation, regardless. But not one major French record company will take the risk. Time and again I would hear those visionless cowards claim that House would be forgotten in six months. So, that left the Disco labels: Happy Music and Scorpio Music. I bring out Darling Mayo's track on Scorpio because of its boss, Henri Bellolo.

Flashback. Ten years earlier

D.I.S.C.O. At the end of the '70s two ambitious young French producers head for the US to make their fortunes, their taste for funky music and business being severely restricted in Giscard d'Estaing's France. Henri Bellolo, a heterosexual Tunisian Jew, knows the language of showbiz, can speak English and talk dollars. His partner, Jacques Morali, a childhood friend, is a composer with a gift for dance music. He's gay and knows inside-out that closet world of bars *à la Cruisin'*. Between them they transform America into one gigantic backroom, thanks to the success of 'YMCA', a hit which Morali composed for the group they manufacture: Village People. For the time, it's the most unbelievable kitsch, camp, queer, delirious, fun band ever seen, and it also appeals to grandmothers and their little boys. 'In the Navy' even turns sailors into popstars. Morali and Bellolo become kings of the world. It's Boogie Nights on all floors. They sell over one hundred million records in five years. Rich and famous, they return to Paris. Later, they will release Patrick Juvet's brilliant disco hit 'Où sont les femmes?', co-written with Jean-Michel Jarre, which charts both sides of the Atlantic. Last night a DJ saved my life.

France invents Disco. Ex-drummer Cerrone creates its beat with 'supernature' and Patrick Hernandez its existentialist philosophy with his mega-hit featuring those unforgettable lyrics, 'Yes I was born, born, born . . . to be alive'. Hernandez benefits from the talents of a young, unknown dancer for his TV shows: Madonna Louise Cicconne. That truly funky designer, Jean Paul Goude, creates disco couture, transforming Grace Jones into Disco queen and superchic fashion diva. *Paris, c'est fou!* In 1979 Le Palace is bought by the legendary Fabrice Emaer, it's the only club which equals New York's Studio 54 for the title of 'the best club in the world'. Grace Jones reigns supreme over the flora and fauna of le Tout Paris, along with Amanda Lear, panties in hand. Move your body.

The Disco years end with the sound of the trio Ottawan's

hit 'D.i.s.c.o.', written by the daddy of Thomas B., the renowned creator twenty years later of those neo-Disco groups and suppliers of planetary hits, Daft Punk and Stardust.

Hip Hop till you drop
South of France. Early '90s

I'm splashed across *Nice-Matin*, the côte d'azur's no. 1 paper, as Ice MC's keyboard player. Ice is a young rapper and ex-breakdance champion from Nottingham. His hip House hit 'Easy', produced in Italy, tops the European charts. We're invited by the organisers of MIDEM, the annual international record fair, to appear on their TV show as part of an all-star line-up. The presenter, Rosie Perez, a petite Puerto Rican bombshell with a perfectly pitched yet husky voice, is Spike Lee's leading lady in his latest, sublime Hip Hop opus *Do The Right Thing*. Techno-tronix 'Pump up the Jam' and we hear backstage gossip that their original singer-dancer recently O-D'd. BlackBox storm it with their mega-hit 'Ride on Time' sampled from Lolleatta Holloway, the Salsoul diva. The lead singer of DJ Daniele Davoli's Italian group is also French. She's dynamite. At the end of the show, I join my mates from the West Coast Hip Hop crew, Digital Under-ground. Their DJ, his name a blank in my brain, is a young white guy from Orlando, and their rapper is a young black guy with a strange name: Tupac Shakur. We hit the Opéra club, but can't get in. Cannes does not welcome young blacks and beurs (arabs). So, instead we run down the Croisette screaming to the sound of the waves, it's great, it reminds the LA crew of California. Have a laugh and split. Back to Hôtel Martinez.

Next day Ice MC is due on at the Whisky à Gogo and I find out I'm fired. Fuck. The group's Italian manager didn't appreciate my stealing the limelight in the local press. The politics of dancing.

That afternoon, I stroll out of the Palais des Festivals record-mart hand-in-hand with Marie, our trio's gorgeous black dancer. We're playing The Superstars. Suddenly, a little guy in glasses springs at me from nowhere. He obviously thinks I'm an American musician. (In the South of France, for American musician read demi-god.) Amused, I let him stutter on in Inspector Clouzeau English and answer in Parisian French. Surprised but pleased, he gives me a tape. He's looking for a producer for the group he's managing: IAM, from the inner-city estates of north Marseille. The little guy swears on the head of the Madonna of the Old Port that they're *gonna be BIII . . . G*. I accept the deal. IAM's lead rapper, Philippe a.k.a. Akenathon, is a visionary. A couple of weeks later I produce two tracks for them with my remixing partners Immense Paris II London. Mix in London. Back to Marseille. The little guy announces in his southern accent that IAM have been signed by Virgin and that he's out of the picture. It's all over. I take the money and run. On the road again.

A few years later IAM hit the jackpot with their single 'Le Mia' which stays at no. 1 in the French charts for several weeks.

Today, they are the most famous of all French Hip Hop groups, the only one which equals Suprème NTM.

NTM (Nique Ta Mère – Motherfucker) is the Word in inner-city estates around Paris and is the no. 1 graffiti known by les Keufs (the pigs). Le Verlan (street slang) is the official language of the kids of '93, an inner-city esperanto. In Saint Denis, home of the Stade de France, NTM are born. Graffiti artists turned rappers, Kool Shen and Joey Starr, the latter a superstar enraged like Goldie, are censored and banned across the board for their radical lyrics. They may scare the shit out of parents, but even without any radio airplay, they still sell millions of CDs for Sony Music. Joey Starr and gorgeous Beatrice Dalle, of *Betty Blue* fame, become for a while the ultimate, legendary, trashy celebrity couple of this *fin-de-siècle*. Radical and chic.

The war between IAM (fighting on the side of Marseille, France's second largest city of France), and NTM (fighting on the side of Paris) is nothing new. North v. South of France. Olympique de Marseille v. Paris Saint Germain. The territorial rivalry between the two posses is like those gangs in NYC and downtown LA warring for supremacy in the Hip Hop community. Bad 2 the bone.

IAM and NTM are the stars of the world's second rap-producing country. The messengers of the inner city, they spread the Word. They spread the culture. They're the Big Brothas of all inner-city kids: blacks, blancs, beurs. Don't fuck with us! A Magnum 357 loaded with words 4 bullets.

Inner-City Life

'Leave your kid to roam 'n he could slip' – NTM, 1998.

Les Cités:* Here it's hate, the ghetto, crack-dealers, kids growing alone because their parents can't deal with them, but, from the age of six, wearing Nike trainers at eighty quid a pair. Designer labels by any means necessary. Poverty creates crime. And crime means guns, not fun. Fear rules OK. France is a country which has always turned her back on the problems of her Cités, leaving her inner-city kids to rot with no other future than illegality. A surreal world in which only the latest Lacoste gives you an identity. The cops stopped going in long ago because they're scared. Gangsters decree the Law, listening to no one, neither parents nor teachers. They racketeer the youngest ones at school and control their own neighbourhoods. The inner city is an island unto itself: a state prison, one big, poor, multiracial community. Born inside the ghetto, you're sentenced to live. There's no escape, you're branded for life. A united state of necessity. But Hip Hop pays. IAM and NTM say it loud and clear: it's about to blow. Their lyrics give hope to the kids who feel alienated from the normal world. Meanwhile, the Parisian music industy

* For la banlieue (with a small b) read the suburbs in general. For la Banlieue (with a capital B) read the poor, working-class neighbourhoods surrounding France's main cities, in which Les Cités were built in the '60s. The largest of these tower-block estates can house up to twenty thousand people. They were created in order to rehouse the inhabitants of the shanty towns which sprang up after World War II and the immigrants from the Maghreb, Africa and the Antilles brought in to France as a source of cheap labour. Once the stronghold of the Communist party, the Front National have recently moved in. Les Cités are similar to the inner cities in the UK and the projects in the USA.

loves it and is busy cashing in on the phenomenal sales of Rap across France.

1998. The inner city wins its first major victory on home ground. At the Stade de France in Saint Denis, it carries off the World Cup. The Stars of the team are Zidane, a beur from the inner-city estates of north Marseille, midfielder for Juventus of Turin and true world-class player, and Thuram, a young African first discovered in the Parisian Banlieue, nominated best foreign player for the Calcio in 1997. That night, millions descended on les Champs Elysées. It's the second Liberation of Paris. The inner-city kids walked tall. 'World Champions', it's something else. My seven-year-old son, Martin Luther, was so happy he cried rivers. The Adidas kids had a big laugh when les Bleus won 3–0. 'Ronaldo! The best player in the World? Truth is, the guy's a joke, a total waste of money.' That night, the Brazilian team and its sponsors, Nike, freaked out. Eighty thousand people in the stadium and the inner-city mob waiting outside. 'If you're shitting yourself, then you can fuck off home to your Mum,' says Little Rachid about the Boys from Brazil. Psalm 3, Epistle 0 of the Gangsta's Gospel. Amen.

Word up 2 Eric le Rouge, *enfant des Caillols de Marseille*, Cyrano of modern football. U were the inspiration.

But it's in the capital that the story of French Hip Hop begins . . .

Paris, 1981

The socialists take power after twenty-seven years of right-wing government. Party time! Jack Lang, Minister of Culture, fashion victim and Mayor of Nancy, becomes aware of the importance of the movement rising up from the street. He forms SOS Racism at the head of which he instals a young guy from the Antilles with a name like a pop star: Harlem Désir. They have a strong slogan: 'Don't touch my pal.' The whole nation picks up on it. This is the first time inner-city language is officially recognised. The President of the French Republic, François Mitterand, red rose in hand, sides with Youth. The Godfather. His protégé, Bernard Tapie, is a fortune-hunter and a businessman. Tonton (Mitterand's nickname: Uncle) offers him l'Olympique de Mar- seilles in exchange for his frankness and street credibility. Tapie, inner-city kid with a preppy look, will win the European Cham- pions Cup as the chairman of l'OM and become a minister. But not, as planned, the Mayor of Marseille. In 1995 when Mitterand dies, Tapie is locked up for fraud, embezzlement and match- fixing. Outsiders are not welcome in French politics. Tapie was the only one ever to talk to the inner cities in their language and probably the first French rapper to become a minister.

But it's 1981, white Rock music rules and Bob Marley is dead.

So funk U!

In Paris a new club opens, at no. 3 Boulevard de Strasbourg, 'hood of whores, junkies and kebab-merchants, 'Chez Roger,

Boite Funk'. Sleazy. It's the first time inner-city life and Parisian showbiz mix. In France, a country rooted in rural tradition, people are wary.

The atmosphere's electric. A skinny white DJ cuts and mixes deadly funk beats. It's the great Dee Nasty. He's from the Cité Bobigny. He's the Man. Hanging out at the bar are the stars of American graffiti art: Phase II and Futura 2000. In town from the Big Apple, we're told they're the best in the world; rumour has it that Keith Haring's jealous to the bone, he who makes millions! They're chatting to Marthe Lagache, stylist, model and graduate of Marie Rucki's Cours Berçot, the college of alternative fashion. Marthe, Queen of the Night, throws the ultimate parties of the '80s. Meanwhile, Hervé Duflot, future boss of the club Sheherazade and of the What's Up Bar, feeds me the latest hot gossip. Look round. Karim and Yasmina let rip to a severely remixed James Brown track. Brothas staring at flirtatious Lolitas create a heavy vibe. Those gorgeous little prick-teasers should've gone to Le Balajo – that gilded monument to café society – to check out DJ Albert, who also reigns over Wednesday nights at London's Café de Paris. Safer, that's for sure.

On stage, Run DMC, real guns in hand, do the human beat box and freak the place out. Public Enemy would play one of their first gigs here. Africa Bambaata would preach here for Zulu Nation. The most feared of all Parisian gangs, the Black Panthers, control security. The temperature's rising. Hip Hop is well at home in Paris, superbly dangerous and wickedly rhythmed by a merciless groove. No one gets out of here alive. Boom!

France. Chaos reigns. Pirate radio stations supported by François Mitterand seem like happy May '68 students' meetings: enthusiastic but skint and broadcasting the mood for change. Radio NRJ rallies hundreds and thousands of young people who hit the street for the largest ever demo organised in the name of Freedom to Listen. Radio NRJ would become the largest, but unfortunately most tedious, of privatised radio stations. The pleasure of listening to good music on the new FM airways is mindblowing – what with 'La Voix du Lezard' (now Skyrock the fourth national radio station), the anarchist-middle-class 'd'Ici et Maintenant', the slick 'Poste Parisien', and hundreds of other new stations springing up each day. But all of Paris tunes in to Radio Nova.

Radio Nova was founded by anti-dandy, ex-hippy, mashed 'n' loaded J. F. Bizot. The son of major industrialists from around Lyons, he owned the paper *Actuel*, which became *Nova* magazine, and invented *la sono mondiale*. No ads – there wouldn't be any on his station for years – few DJ's, but all the latest World Music. Salsa and African music became its trademark. Bizot is always after catching the latest, fashionable thing. He'd even kill his mum 'n' dad to be trendy. So Parisian. Of course, he didn't know much about music, but what with his pal Chris Blackwell, boss of Island Records, and a court of young admirers, he always kept his finger on the pulse. A fox. He got Dee Nasty on board. Dee Nasty's Friday-night show was one hundred per cent underground,

Hip Hop and funky. He first turned people on to Rap and, of course, Radio Nova. La Banlieue was glued to the station.

But it took another ten years before Polydor signed up MC Solaar and Jimmy Jay, and before Hip Hop and Rap got into the Franch charts. The Beat goes on.

The '90s again

I discover Garage. This music from New York gay clubs is an ideal fusion of Soul and House. DJ's Frankie Knuckles and Junior Vasquez, and the producer David Morales, inspire me. I play their remixes at my new club night, 'Radical Chic', held every Friday at Le Sheherazade, rue de Liège. This venue is a magic place, built just after the First World War by an obsessive artist-decorator who locked himself up inside it for a few weeks. It's like a stage-set for *The Thousand and One Nights*. 'Radical Chic' is the first heterosexual Parisian club where the new sound can be heard. It drives girls crazy.

Looking for serious fun. Our hardcore followers are young Brits living in Paris. Seal, Tim Fielding (Journeys by DJ's boss), Johnny Herbert (Formula One driver) and other celebs visit us. The girls come in droves from all around the world. Feral beauties. The drugs are of the finest quality. We rarely sleep before noon. Dan the Man mixes at my side and we occasionally eat caviare after hours with the club's bosses, Hervé and Fred. Patrice Duvallet and Noggin, my partners from Immense Paris II London, help me organise this happy mayhem. Paris just loves to party! Richard Penny, a posh Englishman, trashed as usual, is inspired by our success. He sets up 'Arena', which metamorphoses into 'Soma', a monthly night held at L'Elysée Marbeuf in the 8ème. Laurent Garnier DJ's along with Derrick May, Jerome Pacman and Eren. Competition? Truth is, we're all mates who dance in each other's clubs. One big crazy family.

House is underground. Techno is on its way. Goa Trance takes over. TranceBody take this new breed of ravers to the outermost limits of la Banlieue and into the woods. DJ's from Spiral Tribe and Total Eclipse don't mix vinyls, but play DATs, replete with sounds gleaned from their interstellar trips. LSD-CT.

Once again the major record labels stay deaf to this magnificent call. Immense Paris II London's first 12-inch is released on the London label, Truelove, and hits no. 7 in the UK dance charts. A few months later, Tony Humphries spins our follow-up, 'Come With Me', out on Vinyl Solution, at London's biggest club, the Ministry of Sound.

The furiously gay and only Techno radio station, Radio FG 98.2, relays the addresses of illegal raves and Underground club nights across town, in the face of the cops. Radio FG asserts itself by logo on flyers. It becomes notorious among the tripped-out. Late at night, young guys who want to pull, call the station and talk sex live on air. Happy pornography. In the day, it's a fantastic platform for young French DJs to showcase from.

MC Solaar is all over magazine front-covers. His hit single

'Bouges de là' and the follow up CD make him a social phenomenon and the acceptable face of the inner cities. Immense Paris
II London produces his backing singer Melaaz, but even though
she's loaded with talent, she's too much of a pain. We walk out.
During one of the sessions at the La Bastille recording studio,
Michel Gondry, a musician from the Indie group 'Oui-Oui',
confides in me that he's had enough of being in a band. He now
directs pop promos for the Rolling Stones and Madonna. Wise
move.

Laurent Garnier's new soirée, 'Wake up Paris', at Le Rex
on the Grands Boulevards, is where Parisians first discover Carl
Cox. Le Rex is full to the max every Thursday night. At Le
Queen, David Guetta's reign over Parisian nightlife begins. He
brings over leading DJ's from the US. He and his wife Cathy
are The Couple seen about town. Under their aegis, Le Bataclan,
Le Palace and then Les Bains-Douches become overnight suc-
cesses. Their format is simple and does the trick: part gay, part
trendy, a few celebs, and roll the dice. St Tropez-sur-Seine.

French politics are in turmoil. The legislative elections
result in an unprecedented situation: the Prime Minister and
his government are right-wing and the President socialist. It's
cohabitation. The net is closing around us. The Sheherazade
club is shut down because of 'sound pollution'. So here we are,
homeless again. But not for long.

Le Café Vogue, rue de la Chaussée d'Antin, welcomes our
new soirée: 'Hippy Shake Shake'. A chic club in the 9ème, we

transform it into a Hindu temple, tented and incense-filled. But it's not our patch. Too far away from Pigalle.

Miriam R, my partner, unveils her first fashion show at Le Club d'Arc, near the Champs Elysées. The arrival of our crazy troupe of pranksters in this affluent, uptight club provokes mayhem. The models parade on the lawn and we're all on E. I spin records made of sounds from another world. The clothes are fabulous. Deliciously sexy, just like Miriam R. Her label: Radical Chick.

We got a passion for fashion. Our slogan, 'Created by Immense Paris II London', headlines our flyers.

At the recently reopened ex-bordello-turned-bar, Lili la Tigresse, we stage cabaret-cum-club soirées on Sunday nights. 'Jelly Babys and Peacefull Friends' is a hit. The mix of performers and House, drag queens and dancers dressed by Miriam R, is wild. Hollywood Circus. The Media love it. On the ground floor I mix Disco-House with young Toby, future label manager of The End Records. On the first floor, John Lin, our very own cartoon animator shows incredible 3D visuals and fortune-teller Jean Mi predicts Beatrice Dalle's future. Paris rushes in. For a year, two young guys watch and listen with interest from the corner of the club: Jean-Guy Manuel and Thomas Bangalter, from a new and unknown group called Daft Punk. They give me their first single, recorded round the corner, in their tiny Montmartre studio. Daft Punk, the single, is released on Soma, a Glaswegian label. Immense split up. Long live the Jelly Babys.

—————

Don't sleep till u get enuff! Success hurts. 'Yi King', released on Polygram and the first ever French Ambient album, is our swansong. We go back to Pigalle in search of inspiration.

St Petersburg: I mix for Journeys by DJ. Cannes Film Festival: I mix for Moving Pictures, who hold the most impressive party of the lot at the Château de la Napoule. Paris: Immense Paris II London is history. But long live the Jelly Babys. Our launch: 'Freakout' at l'Espace Cardin, promoted by the newspaper *Libération*, is outrageous. One thousand five hundred party people, high on decibels, lose it in this magical art gallery and drift past streams, pictures, sculptures ... From under a glass menagerie, in which tropical birds fly about, the sky seems so high, so far away. I always wondered if birds like House. South of France: the biggest ever 'legal' rave, 'Boréalis', is staged in the Roman amphitheatre at Nîmes, by les Pingouins, a group from Montpellier. It unites the heavyweights of the House Nation. The authorities authorise, but the CRS riot police are ready and waiting. Ibiza: I DJ in Café Mambo, looking out to sea, and stay in Boy George's villa, where three gorgeous German chicks help me relax by the pool.

Paris: Christophe Audet and Pierre Paparemborde, who run the label GGS, introduce me to Mory Kante, the great African singer who recorded the world hit 'Ye Ké, Ye Ké'. He wants me to produce his next album 'Tatebola'. I've always dreamed of working with him. During the following months I feel as though I'm in Africa. Mory is a holy man. It gives me a chance to forget the superficiality of the club scene and to concentrate on the roots of rhythm.

Funky Paris

At the What's Up Bar, Hervé Duflot introduces a new sound, Trip Hop, and DJ Cam is flavour of the month in pop-art magazines *Technickart* and *Les Inrockuptibles*. Omnisonus, the first Parisian Techno label, brings out records by young French DJs, Jerome Pacman, Djulz and DJ Sonic. My mate, Jef K, releases a compilation with Distance Records, an independent House label, and becomes the most wanted DJ in France. Dimitri, a DJ from Radio NRJ, metamorphoses into 'Dimitri from Paris'. His album 'Sacrébleu' makes of him an international star. It could've been Patrick Vidal, the original French Disco DJ, but Dimitri did it. The big boys are beginning to get the drift.

Motorbass and Cassius are the brainchild of Philippe Zdar and Pigalle Boom Bass, the sons of the no. 1 French sound engineer of the '70s, Dominic Blanc Francart, who recorded three of Elton John's albums at le Château d'Hérouville. They're also MC Solaar's producers. Their music swings from House to Hip Hop. One of the same skool, Etienne de Crécy, masterminds the album 'Super Discount'. Daft Punk are signed by Virgin France. They teach French music business a lesson in hype. Before their first album's released, Virgin moves up a gear. The majors rake it in. They forget to thank us in the underground. What's new?

Christov Rühn a.k.a. DJ Tov

The Jelly Babys inaugurate 'Zoom' at la Bastille. Deliberately cosy, 'Zoom' is a club night for our close friends, an intimate space embellished to the smallest detail. Two hundred people trip out every Thursday. Eurostar invite us to create our own tent at the second festival of Richard Branson's label V2 in Chelmsford. Zoom Paris. Drugs Paris. Natural-born aliens. Miriam R launches her new collection of combat-wear at Le Palace, the night before its official closure. This mysterious shutdown implicates the most eminent leaders of State. It hasn't reopened since. *Le fric c'est pas toujours très chic.*

'Zoom' is over. Our last celebration is held at the What's Up Bar for Christmas. Love don't live here any more. It's nearly a year since I've made music. I dream of the most beautiful club in the world. Our rivals, the underground promoters Magic Garden, take over Le Bataclan in Boulevard Voltaire. Then I get a call from my friend Stéphanie D. She has Floflo, the PR for Elysée Montmartre, on the other line, looking for club promoters.

One month later, the Jelly Babys are on at l'Elysée Montmartre. The party is called 'Fantazzia'. The Jelly Babys are down to three members only: Miriam, 504 and me. We're given a major budget. The ballroom, built by Eiffel for l'Exposition Universelle in 1900, becomes the theatre of our dreams. We build a Palace of Space, misty with lacey veils, swathed in metallic gold fabric, and with gigantic transparent balloons, held by invisible threads. Miriam dresses the dancers Anoushka and Sonia in sexy Paco Rabanne-style warrior outfits. They dance behind a

3×4-metre screen on to which the experimental artists Human Technology generate 3D images thanks to a revolutionary computer programme. Blade from the Italian group Jestofunk and Robert Owens join me on the decks. OldSkool DJs from all over the world, and Cece Rogers on the mike, help to create a hallucinatory atmosphere. Until June, the Jelly Babys rule over Paris. The last soirée takes place with guest Armand Van Helden. Curtain.

Our other rivals, Jérome Vigier from FG Radio FG 98·2, David Blot from Radio Nova and Fred Antonini, launch 'Respect' at Le Queen. Their idea to invite DJs and promoters from overseas for a midweek club night is a success. Daft Punk kick off the opening party, along with Dimitri from Paris, Philippe Zdar from Motorbass, les Idjut Boys . . .

Independent labels are flourishing. French House is mainstream. The melodies of Air invade the world. And I'm bored. I leave everything behind and head for new horizons. Tomorrow is another day. And I'm still alive. Just.

Lost in Music.

FIN

Love 2 my mum (she is the one who can write) and dad, my brother and sisters. Peace 2 Immense, Jelly Babys and all my peaceful friends, wherever they might be, this is your story too. Hélène and Lee, U R

_____

my family. Special mention 2 my London friends, Meredith and Christian, Raz, Boo, Torty and Nigel, Guy, Simon and Jan, Matthew J and Linzi for their unconditional support, a very big merci 2 Jonathan P (I stole his sox for 6 months and wrote this story on his computer, cheers mate!), the beautiful women of the world (they know who they are) 4 inspiration and finally thanx 2 Justin Laurie (we can do it, bro!), my agent Georgia de C. @ BookBlast who literally threw me into this . . . Sorry but I could not mention all of U.

Marcel Desailly

Champions du Monde

Marcel Desailly

The French team won the World Cup in front of two billion TV viewers, infinitely more spectators than when Man first walked on the moon. Would you like to walk on the moon?

(*laughter*) Of course, walking on the moon was an exceptional event, a technological breakthrough. Today, football gets a huge amount of media coverage and to be an actor in front of all those people is great. You should make the most of it!

Djorkaeff declared in an interview that this particular French team will make the pages of history. What do you think?

So it seems, yes, I think I will. After France was knocked out of the '94 World Cup qualifications, we went on to win a whole run of matches. This had never happened before. We reached the semi-finals of Euro '96 and then went on to win the '98 World Cup. This generation of players is made to last and is hungry for results, in both Euro 2000 and World Cup 2002, the two major events to come. We really have the strength and the spirit, making us feel we can achieve something exceptional every time.

Is France the favourite for Euro 2000?

Yes, certainly. Since Brazil, Argentina and the other South American teams will not be competing, this leaves us with a pretty good chance to go all the way. Germany and Holland are also serious contenders, but since we were crowned world champions last year, it's normal that we should be the team to beat and finish amongst the top three.

How did you feel at 0–1 down against Croatia during the semi-finals of the World Cup?

Lousy, because we could see ourselves already there, in the final, and we never even imagined falling on the last step. Anxious also, since we'd always been the first to score in previous matches, so we were disoriented to find ourselves down 1–0 at half-time. At the beginning of the second half we were relieved when Thuram did a mad one and equalized, so we didn't have a chance to get scared, though for a brief moment the pressure got to us, we had doubts.

Was it the first time you were behind since the beginning of the tournament?
Yes, and at this point we were feeling so strong and confident, especially at the back, in defence, and suddenly everything was turned upside down.

Can the stress of a big game become a plus at certain crucial moments, in the case of a penalty shoot-out for example? Do you ever take part in penalty shoot-outs?
I'm usually one of the last ones to do so. It's a highly stressful moment, one that you never get used to, in that the bigger the match the greater the stress and we have to stay positive, give our best. We love to play big games. The fear of a penalty miss during a shoot-out is the worst. You only get one try and that's it. In a match situation you can always miss one or two passes and get back into position, back into the game, but in this case, it's a matter of seconds, period. It's a negative type of stress and hard to deal with.

Would you say that friendship amongst the players of a team is an important factor towards achieving victory?
Not necessarily. Before the World Cup, the coach brought us together in Tignes so the team could connect properly, because at that point we had mutual respect for each other, but that was about it. When you spend your professional life in the eye of the media or as part of a group with a major goal to achieve, and the stakes are high, becoming true friends is all down to results. Today, having won the World Cup and lived such an incredible adventure together, there's a strong emotional bond between us. We've become friends, which should propel us towards even greater success, and we've

consolidated links. We've had some great moments together and we don't want to stop. Now, on the pitch, if one of us finds himself in a difficult situation, there's always somebody there to help him out.

How great an advantage was it to play the World Cup in France? Did it help you win the championship?
It gave us a major advantage, certainly. It's not the same game when a side plays at home or plays away. In '84 France also won the European Championship at home. It's a great advantage.

Has France developed any special training skills or tactics which makes it a better side than all the other national teams?
Tactically, nothing is new. We usually play a 4/2 . . . (*pause*) a 4/3/2, wait a minute, a 4/3/2, what am I saying, one's missing! . . . (*laughter*) . . . a 4/3/3. France uses a straightforward system. At the beginning of Euro '96 Aimé Jacquet used three holding midfielders: Vincent Guérin, Christian Karembeu on the right-hand side and Didier Deschamps in the middle, they were on top form, it was a revelation which worked well for us. The team based itself around those tactics, with three holding midfielders and four defenders backing them up, so we gained confidence from that moment on. It gave us sheer strength and made us tougher. During the World Cup, the coach changed the team's tactics and used only two holding midfielders, Didier Deschamps and Emmanuel Petit, making it a more attacking side. Jacquet's main talent was to change the system as we went along, at just the right moment, to make the side stronger, more aggressive, more powerful. For the final, he went back to three midfielders: Christian Karembeu on the right-hand side to stop Roberto Carlos, Didier Deschamps in a central position in charge of Rivaldo, and Petit on the left. The coach's vision is vital, as are the team's tactics, but Jacquet didn't bring anything revolutionary to the game.

Do you still get anxious about being called up for selection?
No . . . (*laughter*). Maybe, one day if I don't have a good season and I realize there's some young player coming up behind me . . . but right now, no, I'm not worried at all.

How do you find time to train when you play matches almost every three days?
We train very little, we do warm-ups, we throw the ball at each other. We don't have much spare time for proper training. In fact it's better that way. We'd rather play competitions, than train during the week, and conclude on matches. Anyway, we're usually fit enough when we play every three days, so training is more about recovery.

You haven't been injured that often?
Being a defender isn't as risky as playing forward and I've been lucky enough to avoid injuries during my career.

Why have you so rarely accepted the captaincy of the teams you've played for?
It's not really our choice, it's up to the coach to decide. The captain is usually the most capped player, or sometimes it's the one who's a natural-born leader. I'm third on the list, just after Laurent Blanc and Didier Deschamps. Clubwise, I was often Nantes' captain, but not Marseille's – I was a young player and had just landed at the club – and Milan had Baresi. Here at Chelsea I'm one of the new boys. We need someone who's already well integrated within the club, someone who can speak to the press and to the club's chairman.

To be or not to be a star, is it a choice?
It can become a choice. You can always keep a low profile and do your job quietly, without putting yourself forward, without giving interviews. You'll still remain somebody important in

the public's heart, regardless. But a star, I'm not sure. I believe it's a personal choice.

Are you a star?
No, but I've sometimes had a message to get across.

Does playing for your country and being a world champion make you feel French first and foremost?
It's clear that I'm a Frenchman, with a wide-ranging European culture, in that I've lived here for a longer period of time than in Africa, but my origins are African and that's something I'll never forget. France gave me the opportunity to defend its colours, I'll always do the best I can, but my roots are my roots. I forget nothing.

Isn't there something sad and ridiculous about certain ill-advised politicians thinking they had the right to put down the French national team because it wouldn't always sing the national anthem before matches, when, for once, and thanks to this very team, the young people of France from every horizon, who are its real future, could at last feel truly French?
In '96 Jean-Marie Le Pen commented on this. It would've been wrong for us to give it too much significance. He wanted to point out the fact that a lot of players were of Moroccan, Algerian, African, and New-Caledonian descent, but France is a very mixed country due to its former colonies. Jean-Marie Le Pen would've probably liked a French national team only to be made up of players who bore a French pedigree, but that's not very realistic. The players didn't care much anyway. We were more disturbed by the fact that the media made an issue of it and therefore some people tried to make things difficult for us. Ultimately, it didn't really bother us at all.

Many French players now play for some of Europe's biggest clubs. Which came first, the chicken or the egg?

Before, when French players went to major European clubs, it was usually on a trial basis, but now they definitely make those sides stronger, they bring with them their experience, their knowledge of the game. It's a good think for French football. At Milan I adapted quickly tactically, since there are few cultural differences between the two countries. I adjusted as well as any other player before me, and the fact that I had an oustanding first season helped, it was great. Tant mieux.

Certain big managers have declared to the press that the future of football lies in a clubs' rather than a national teams' World Cup. What are your views?
I disagree, you play for your country, for your flag.

How do you feel about the fact that French youth, which looks up to you, only rarely gets a chance to see its favourite star players elsewhere than on TV?
Today football is big business, that's the reality. A player will go abroad if he thinks he'll be better off, get even greater recognition, and that it's a good career move; it's the system that's responsible for this. France isn't attractive enough financially to keep its best players. It hasn't got what it takes.

At Milan you gave numerous interviews to the press, why don't you do the same at Chelsea?
Precisely because I gave a lot of interviews when I played for Milan, so when I got to Chelsea, I was tired of it all. I want to be able to go home at night without having too much on my mind. If journalists want to write about me, let them, but I'm not that keen on it. I might change my mind later on, when I feel more settled in this country.

The tabloid press is frequently cruel. Would you rather read books?
No, unfortunately, I don't read books, I read the news and anything to do with finance. I don't read books because I

never manage to take enough time out from football to discover reading. I don't read the tabloids either.

Are Italy, England and Spain promised lands for players looking for recognition, glory and money?
Yes, those three countries are the ones.

You've stated that British football is too aggressive. Do you think that French players have been bought by Premiership clubs to bring in flair and a touch of magic?
Whether we're talking about the Italian players here at Chelsea or the French at other Premiership clubs, I believe that's true in that both Serie A and the French championnat are renowned for being more tactically skillful than the Premier League. The Premiership is rather limited in this respect, but there's considerable physical involvement on the pitch. At times it's too aggressive and the referees let the game play on, so it can become dangerous. Seen from the inside, I'm surprised and dismayed by this so-called fighting spirit.

Playing at Wembley while living and working in England must be a strange experience. How did you feel before and especially after the '99 England v France fixture?
Wembley was never mythical for me. I only knew the stadium through rugby, since I'm interested in it, and FA cup finals. Before I became a Chelsea player I didn't pay much attention to the Premiership. The other players in the French national team raved on about Wembley's legendary status. To me, it's a stadium like any other, where I was going to play a big match, participate in a major event. The 2–0 win was pleasurable, and the next morning we showed up at the club smoking fat cigars, it was fun.

How do you keep calm when you're constantly being challenged on the pitch? Does England live up to its fair-play image?

No, and I'm beginning to realize this every day. I thought there'd be more of it. The only time fair play really seems to exist is during the televised finals, because the Queen or a member of the Royal family is sitting in the Royal box, and this restrains players from making provocative gestures. The rest of the time, during ordinary games, you end up more often than not on your arse.

It isn't always easy living in the UK if you're Black. What's it like for you: a champion who's Black, French and playing for an English club?
London is such a cosmopolitan city that the way people look at you is different to the way they do in France. For a Black in France, every time you go into a shop you're scrutinised by zealous assistants curious to know what you want, what you're up to, what shoes you're wearing, how you're dressed, as a way of assessing your status. Here, it seems to be better. From the age of around fifteen–seventeen, since I was becoming known as a football player, it helped to cool people off. In truth, I haven't experienced that much racism or sensed people giving me sidelong glances. In football everybody is so used to being with players from different races, from various horizons and countries, that being Black doesn't make you feel like an outcast, as is the case in so many other jobs; it's OK. There seems to be less racism in the Premiership than in Italy or France.

As an African, one day, would you like to bring your expertise to an African club, for them to win a much coveted World Cup trophy?
Unfortunately, I never had it in me, I don't have the vocation necessary to become a coach and can't see myself doing it. I've been an actor in this game for many years, and I don't want to go on having to live under such stress. I might be tempted to train children up to the age of twelve or thirteen because it's less demanding, and this way maybe I could give back to

football something of what football has given me. Being a coach, I'd resent not being able to express myself on the pitch, I'd have to watch rather than act. Football has always been and remains my true passion, but there are, after all, a million and one other things to do in life. Once I've stopped my career . . . no doubt I'll end up helping out kids.

Is the excessive amount of money in football today a snare or a motivator for young people living in the suburbs and inner cities?
It's a snare, given that only very few players actually make it to the top, but it's also positive since it motivates young people to get into sport rather than going off and getting into trouble. Whether it's football, basketball, athletics . . . sport often brings out the best in kids, and a sense of self-worth. It teaches commitment, hard work and willpower. All the same, you've got to be realistic, those who think it's an easy ride should remember that not everybody succeeds.

Did you envisage a career as a footballer ever since you were a child?
Yes, as far as I can remember. When I started at FC Nantes around the age of eight it was just for fun, but when I reached the age of thirteen/fourteen, I began to train regularly with players at the youth academy. I realized I could do something in football.

Today, kids emulate Desailly or Zidane when playing football in the playground. Who were your childhood heroes?
Back then, my heroes were Maradona, Berndt Schuster, Kempes, Johnny Rep, Cruyff. I didn't really have any role-models outside football other than tennis players like McEnroe and Borg, but that's about it. I loved tennis, I was a natural and almost went into it professionally. The reason I didn't was because it's such a solitary sport, I hated being stuck on my

own with a teacher shouting at me, having to hit the ball again and again. Anyway, team sports were always my favourites.

What do Keegan and Platini symbolize to you, now that you're more famous than they are?

I wouldn't say that, no, not more famous. I might have won more honours than they have, but you should take into account that I'm one of a new generation of players and the notions are different. We may be players of quality, but we're not as special as they were. No doubt I'm a good centre-back but those guys had something more, they were creators. Me, I'm a defender. There's no way you can make any sort of comparison with them because they played in a different era. Platini is the French player of the century and it's hard for anybody to even get close to his level. Alone, he carried both the French national team and Juventus of Turin.

You're possibly the best central defender in the world. Does this provoke jealousy?

I've tried to keep a grip on simplicity and not let anything get to me. I'm not like I used to be when I was around twenty-three or twenty-four: a crazy young player constantly in search of glory, trying to come out looking better than everyone else.

How did you feel when you were sent off in the World Cup final?

I felt disappointed and a bit scared. Fear, in the first place, because I was aware of having made a very serious mistake. Until then, we were 2–0 ahead and the match was running smoothly, it was something of a sure win. When I got sent off, suddenly everything changed: Brazil had a chance to come back. If things had gone wrong I'd've been the one blamed for it. I was terrified, but ultimately, I never lost confidence in my mates' ability to keep the result. If you watch the video, you'll see I didn't wait for the referee to give me a red card. I said to myself: 'Leave the pitch now, so your team-mates aren't unsettled, so the game can go on'. I didn't want to feel responsible for creating a situation whereby everybody would start to argue and fight all over the place. Of course, back in the changing rooms, it was terrible, waiting for the match to end, not knowing if we'd hold out.

How can you still be so motivated when you've won nearly everything a footballer could ever dream of?
I'd put it down to passion. Sure, I've won the Champions League several times, as well as a few Intercontinental Cups, but I continue to be as passionate as ever about football. After the World Cup, I was confused and doubtful. I questioned my future. It soon became clear tht I needed a change of setting, so I left Milan to go to Chelsea where a new challenge awaited me. The time was right for me to prove my worth to new people, to get motivated again. If I'd stayed with Milan, I'd've probably ended up feeling downhearted, though maybe not to the point of stopping my career.

How important is water in a sportsman's life?
Water is crucial. We're supposed to drink four litres of water a day, whether we have a match to play or not. We use water to recuperate, to rehydrate ourselves and obviously we shower a lot.

Do you believe in luck? And what about love?
Luck has played an important role in my getting to where I am now. And as for love, well, of course I have a wonderful wife and three children.

Today, women seem to love football. Do you think they should get more involved in the game, for example as referees or as managers?
Football is still quite a macho game, it'd be hard for certain people to accept the idea of a woman running a club or as a

central referee. Change isn't for tomorrow, even if there are
already a few female line referees out there. You get the
impression that somehow it'd be easier to take advantage of a
woman referee and that she'd be more likely to lose the plot.
Men are tougher, especially during high-pressure matches.

And what about women's football?
Women's football is of quality and I often go to watch the
French team play, it's always a pleasure. They deserve respect,
even though they aren't talked about enough in the media.
Football is their passion too.

*Footballers sometimes move like dancers. Do you enjoy
listening to music?*
I love Soul, New Jack Swing, R'n'B and occasionally pop . . .
groups like TLC . . . and I've always been a fan of Michael
Jackson. He's one of the planet's greatest stars and he started
out very young.

Who said: 'Que sème le vent récolte le tempo'?
MC Solaar.

*Your list of honours is fabulous. Do you realize that
you'll be a point of reference in football and revered as a
legend for many years to come?*
It's hard for me to say, but yes, certainly as one of the French
national team which won the '98 World Cup. I can't see
Marcel Desailly being remembered as one of the guys who
changed the face of French football.

*Do you believe that, today, footballers are more famous
than Jesus Christ?*
(*laughter*) Well . . . let's put it this way, today in Brazil, people
probably discuss Ronaldo more than Jesus Christ, but it's
impossible to attempt making such a comparison. The French
internationals don't quite realise how famous they are, or the

real impact of their World Cup victory on the public. We're separated from the fans, we don't celebrate with them, we live in a cocoon, as a group focused on achieving a goal. It's beyond us even to begin to appreciate the effect of our victory on people's lives. Perhaps the closest we get is through some of the letters we receive from fans or when we meet them.

Marseille or Milan?

Milan definitely lies in the past, but Olympique de Marseille, who knows? I'm building a house in the South of France, so you should never say never . . .

Is football the new opium for the people?

Sure, I guess so. Football is on the rise, it's getting an increasingly high profile – financially, on TV, across the media, and it hasn't even peaked yet. The world's most famous footballer, Ronaldo, barely earns even a tenth of what the American basketball player, Michael Jordan, makes in earnings and endorsements. Football is the most popular sport on the planet by far, and there's a huge margin for monetary growth. Clubs will be floated on the stockmarkets, there'll be more and more investment in the game. This said, money must not become the only driving force behind football, because, (as is the case in most sports), profits only benefit the professionals, leaving amateur football, a key source of future players, to struggle on as best it can.

Contributors

Marie Desplechin was born in Paris. The phenomenal appeal of her writing to a generation of thirtysomething French women is comparable to that of Helen Fielding's with *Bridget Jones's Diary*. Desplechin is a militant optimist and an astute observer of everyday life. 'She writes with a British touch of humour, mischief and precision, enough to arouse the doziest of readers' (*Le Point*). Her collection of stories *Trop sensibles* topped the bestseller lists and her novel *Sans moi* has sold over 110,000 copies.

Virginie Despentes was born in Nancy. Hardcore grunge babe, she left home aged seventeen and wound up in Lyons. Her novels, *Baise-moi* and *Les chiennes savantes* (written on her Dad's computer without him realising), caused a sensation. Initially spotted by a sharp young publisher, Florent-Massot, her novels now sell by the truckload and she has become a cult figure. Her latest novel, *Les jolies choses*, was released by a mainstream publisher. 'Violent and magnificent' (*Elle*), her heroines a.k.a. Thelma and Louise on the road survive by the only means available to them: sex, hustling and murder. 'Virginie Despentes comes closest to being the one and only French equivalent to Irvine Welsh' (*Les Inrockuptibles*).

Tonino Benacquista was born in Choisy-le-Roi to Italian parents. He writes 'with the melancholy of the completely socially-integrated child of immigrants, all the while acknowledging his roots' (*Libération*). TV script-writer and cartoonist, his novels include: *La maldonne des sleepings, Trois carrès rouges sur fond noir* (Le Trophée 813 du Meilleur Roman Policier, 1990), *La commedia des ratés* (The Grand Prix de la Littérature Policiére & Le Trophée 813 du Meilleur Roman Policier, 1991), *Les morsures de l'aube*, which is being adapted into a feature film by Antoine de Caunes, and *Saga*. 'Benacquista is fabulous . . . If he were translated into English he would be hailed as a miraculous discovery' (*Vogue*)

Michel Houellebecq was born on the island of Réunion in the Indian Ocean and grew up in France. '*Le Prince du supermarché*', he rants against the mediocrity and banality of technological, mass-consumer society, 'the new religion', and exposes the failure of '60s sexual liberalism. 'Novelist of depression and poet of despair', (*Télérama*), his vision is so singular that following the publication of his works, *Rester vivant, La poursuite du bonheur, Le sens du combat* (Prix Flore, 1996), *Extension de domaine de la lutte* and *Les particules élémentaires* (Prix Novembre, 1998 & Prix du Meilleur Livre de l'Année RTL-Lire, 1998) the adjective '*Houellebecquien*' entered the French language. He and a group of fellow writers, notably Nicolas Bourriaud, Eric Holder and Christophe Duchatelet, hang out in a bar, Les Maronniers, in the 4ième arrondissement, where they hold court. Their magazine *Les Perpendiculaires* has made a huge impact on contemporary

Contributors

French writing. 'Le Nouveau Roman focused on the object, on the object's existence. Then, we were surrounded by objects, now, we're surrounded by products and brand-names' (Nicolas Bourriaud).

Guillaume Dustan divides his time between Radio FG 98.2, the magazine *e-m@le* and running a publishing imprint which specialises in gay writing. His name is a pseudonym. His incisive, hardcore novels *Dans ma chambre, Je sors ce soir* and *Plus fort que moi* read like the poignant diary of a sex junkie lost in clubland. 'The greatest writer of this fin de siècle . . . the prophet of the next millenium' (*Technikart*), Dustan puts literary icons Jean Genet, Hervé Guibert and Brett Easton Ellis in the shade.

Agnès Desarthe was born in Paris. She is of Romanian and Libyan descent. A translator (into English) and writer of children's books, her first novel, *Quelques minutes de bonheur absolu*, received the Prix Jeune Ecrivain de la Fondation Hachette. Over 65,000 copies of her second novel, *Un secret sans importance*, sold in France alone, and it was awarded the Prix du Livre Interallié, 1996. Her writing pinpoints 'the universe of suffering and joy thereby giving it international appeal' (*l'Arche*). She has been compared to Alice Thomas Ellis and Isaac Bashevis Singer.

Contributors

Lorette Nobécourt grew up in Paris in a traditional, catholic milieu. She is one of a disparate group of writers – Marie Darrieussecq, Virginie Despentes, Christine Angot, Régine Detambel – who put the female body, its anguish and its metamorphosis, at the centre of their writing. Her novels *La démangeaison* and *La conversation* are tormented monologues exploding with 'madness, despair, searing rebelliousness and screaming rage' (*l'Express*).

Mehdi Belhaj Kacem left Tunisia at the age of thirteen. The voice of the European Generation X of the '90s, MBK is wild and experimental, 'he writes like a devil, plays with and delights in words . . . a violent novelist' (*Le nouvel observateur*). First published at the age of seventeen, his novels *Cancer, 1993, Vies et morts d'Iréne Lepic* and *l'Antéforme* have a cult following. The chaos, violence, alienation, perverse sex and chemical onslaught experienced by his narrators are not symptomatic of youthful rebellion but are endemic in society. 'People appear to see me as some sort of terrorist, representing the Hezbollah branch of literature . . .' (MBK in conversation with David Bowie, *Les Inrockuptibles*).

Frédéric Beigbeder is a columnist for *Voici* and has also written for *Glamour*, *Globe* and *Figaro Magazine*. He regularly collaborates on the TV talk show 'Rive Droite, Rive Gauche'. Published works include: *Mémoires d'un jeune dérangé, L'Amour* *dure trois ans* and *Vacances dans le coma*, in which he satirises trendy Parisian café society out clubbing 'n' drugging. 'Talented and skillful, [he has] savoir-faire, is artful and most of all, has a certain natural, youthful candour' (*Le nouvel observateur*).

Eric Faye grew up in the Limousin and now works for Reuters. Critic and essayist, his published works include: *Ismaïl Kadaré: Prométhée porte-feu, Dans les laboratoires du pire* (a study of totalitarianism and utopia in literature), *Le sanatorium des malades du temps* (a collection of essays on Julien Gracq, Dino Buzzati, Thomas Mann and Kôbô Abé), *Le mystère des trois frontières, Je suis le gardien du phare* (Prix des Deux Magots, 1998) and *Croisière en mer des pluies*. Faye edited the special 1996 issue of *Autrement* dedicated to Kafka. Lost utopias and the death of ideals underpin his imaginative and poetic novels: *Le général solitude* (Prix Cino del Duca, 1996) and *Parij* (Prix Littéraire du Quartier Latin, 1997 & Prix Gironde du Deuxième Roman, 1998). 'From the ashes of socialist realism, Faye has created a new genre: fantastical realism' (*Télérama*).

Vincent Ravalec was born in the Parisian suburbs. Writer and film-maker, he recently founded his own production company. '*Un voyou chic*' (*l'Express*), he was discovered by legendary editor Françoise Verny. An 'exuberant, lewd, uncompromising bard of youth' (*Le Monde*), his collections of stories, *Un pur* *moment de rock 'n' roll*, *Les clés du bonheur*, *Vol de sucettes* and *Recel de bâtons* and his novels, *Cantique de la racaille* (Prix Flore, 1994), *Wendy and Nostalgie de la magie noire* vividly bring alive low life, high life, city life.

Ilan Duran Cohen was born in Jerusalem, grew up in Paris, and went to film school at New York University. Novelist and script-writer, in his autobiographical novel, *Chronique Alicienne*, he makes the territory of Paul Auster and Woody Allen his own. 'He blends, with piquant irony and angsty scepticism, the essential themes of identity, exile, death, friendship, cinema etc. . . . in this funny, rhythmic, subtle, profound, despairing, first novel. Great stuff!' (*Les Inrockuptibles*).

Abdourahmann Waberi was born in Djibouti on the horn of Africa and moved to France in 1985. He currently teaches English at Evreux. His collections of stories, *Le pays sans ombre* (Prix Albert-Bernard, 1994), *Cahier nomade* (Grand Prix Littéraire de l'Afrique Noire, 1996) and a political novel, *Balbala* (Prix Biennal: 'mandat pour la liberté', 1998) form a trilogy about his homeland. 'His writing is highly original, combining myth and poetry . . . with a geographical sense of place and soaring towards a greater universality' (*Les Inrockuptibles*).

Mounsi was born in Kabylie, Algeria and moved to the

industrial Parisian suburb, Nanterre, as a child. Singer and novelist, Mounsi is the Hubert Selby Jnr of contemporary French writing. The fate of delinquents surviving in a brutal universe is brought to life by this 'hugely talented survivor of the wastelands and concrete subterranea of la Banlieue' (*Télérama*) in a style that is 'vivid, passionate and imbued with the seedy, melancholic resonance of the Blues' (*l'Evénement du Jeudi*). Published works include: *La cendre des villes*, *Territoire d'outre-ville*, *Ballade électrique*, *Le Voyage des âmes* and *La Noce des fous*.

Mathieu Lindon is the son of the founder of Les Editions de Minuit. He writes for the books pages of *Libération*. His published works include: *Le livre de Jim Courage*, *Prince et Leonardours*, *l'Homme dui vomit*, *Le coeur de To*, *Champion du monde*, *Merci* and *Les apeurés*. His latest novel, *Le procès de Jean-Marie Le Pen*, an exposure of the extreme right wing party Front National, caused a furore in the French media and shall be at the centre of a human rights case at the European court, Brussels.

Mathieu Kassovitz was born into a family of film-makers. He is one of a group of young directors – Ahmed Bouchaala, Jean-François Richet, Jean-Michel Carré, Karim Dridi and Thomas Gilou – who caused an uproar at the '95 Cannes film festival with their films, which portrayed a side of urban life hitherto denied and shunned by the French establishment. In 1993, seventeen-year-old Makomé Bowole was shot by the *inspecteur de police* at a police station in the 18ième arrondissement, provoking wide-scale rioting in the nearby inner city estate. This incident inspired Kassovitz's cult film, *La Haine*, which received two Césars and the Best Director award. It provoked a national debate across the media and became a box-office hit both at home and abroad. Eleven French Raï, Rap and Hip Hop stars (Cheb Khaled, MC Solaar, IAM etc . . .) released an accompanying CD. Kassovitz's other films include *Métisse* and *Assassin* and he has had a book of poetry published, *Crâme pas les blasés*.

Christov Rühn a.k.a. DJ Tov was nominated the best under-thirteen football player for the Ile de France region in the late '70s and passed the entrance trials for a place at the National Institute of Football. Because of a knee injury he had to stop playing at the age of sixteen. He turned to music, his other passion, and moved to London to learn his trade, where he stayed for five years before returning to Paris. Avant-garde DJ and producer, Christov has worked with the likes of Mory Kante, the African singer best known for his worldwide hit 'Yé Ké Yé Ké', IAM, the number one Hip Hop group from Marseille, Judge Jules, Roy the Roach, Charlie Hall from the Drum Club and many others . . . He was the first DJ to introduce Garage music to Paris, circa 1992. He influenced the local fresh funkhouse scene, Daft Punk and Stardust, with the regular clubs he hosted in the French capital – 'Radical Chic', 'Zoom', 'Jelly Babys', 'Funky People' and 'Fantazzia' – inviting and spinning alongside Armand Van Helden, CeCe Rogers, Robert Owens, Blade (Jestofunk), Laurent Garnier, Keoki ... He recently left Paris to settle in London, where he's composing a new album and working on his first book. He supports Olympique de Marseille and Arsenal.

Marcel Desailly was born in Accra, Ghana, and grew up in France. He began his football career at an early age and has played for Nantes, Olympique de Marseille and Milan. He was the first ever French player to win the Champions' League two years in a row, for two different clubs in two different countries. A world-class defender, he played a major role in France's victory in the '98 World Cup. He now plays for Chelsea FC, where he's nicknamed 'the rock'.

Translators

'No problem is as completely concordant with literature and with the modest mystery of literature as is the problem posed by translation'
J. L. Borges

Boris Belay is a young writer, translator and university lecturer. He has written articles about Derrida, Lacan, Bataille, Sartre and Merleau-Ponty as well as translating critiques of their work, published in the US and France. He taught philosophy at IU Bloomington and SUNY Stony Brook in the States and currently teaches English literature at l'Université de Paris XIII, Villetaneuse. In 1998, he co-authored with Mehdi Belhaj Kacem, *Main basse sur le signifiant*, published by *Le Monde* in a special insert, *31 écrivains face à la haine*.

Steve Cox has translated a wide variety of French authors, including Raymond Aron, Philippe Curval, Philippe Erlanger, Simon Leys and Tony Cartano.

Michael Dash is professor of francophone literature at the University of the West Indies, Jamaica. His published works include *Jacques Stéphène Alexis*, *Literature and Ideology in Haiti*, *Edouard Glissant*, *Haiti and the US* and *The Other America: Caribbean Literature in a New World Context*. He has translated the works of various French-Caribbean writers and *The Village Voice* nominated his translation of Glissant's *Caribbean Discourse* as one of their Books of the Year in 1989.

Translators

Christine Donougher's translation of Sylvie Germain's *The Book of Nights* won the *TLS* Scott Moncrieff Translation Prize in 1992. Other authors she has translated include Jan Potocki, Octave Mirbeau, Marcel Béalu and Rezvani. She is currently working on Sylvie Germain's latest novel, *Tobie des marais*. She lives in Venice.

Paul Hammond is a writer, painter and translator living in Barcelona. Published works include *L'Age d'or* for the BFI, and an essay on the Buñuel documentary *Tierra sin pan*. Translated works include *Constellations of Mirô–Breton*, a compilation of Surrealist film writing, *The Shadow and its Shadow*, and Mônica Gili's new tome on tombs, *The Last House*.

Will Hobson is a contributing editor to Granta magazine and writes a weekly column, 'Hobson's Choice', for the *Independent on Sunday*. His translation of *Viramma, Life of an Untouchable* was published in 1997 and he is currently completing work on Patrick Rambaud's Goncourt-winning novel *La Bataille*.

William Rodarmor, deputy editor of *California Monthly*, has translated ten books from French including works by Agustin Gomez-Arcos, Denis Belloc, Cyril Collard and Christian Lehmann. His translation of Bernard Moitessier's *Tamata and the Alliance* received the 1996 Lewis Galantière Award from

Translators

the American Translator's Association. He lives in Berkeley, California.

Brad Rumph grew up in Washington DC and moved to New York. In 1985 he went to Paris on a cultural roller-coaster and hasn't looked back since.

Ros Schwartz was thrown out of university in the UK in the early '70s. She fled to Paris where she studied at Vincennes, the radical university born out of the student riots of May '68. In 1979, Ros embarked on a career translating works of fiction and non-fiction by contemporary French authors, they include: Sembène Ousmane, Fettouma Touati, Sèbastien Japrisot, Andrée Chedid, Jacqueline Harpmann, Mazarine Pingeot, Catherine Clément and Yasmina Khadra.

Copyright Details

Marie Desplechin

Haiku is taken from the novella *Yûgen (Mystère inéffable)* published in the collection *Trop sensibles*. Published by kind permission of Editions du Seuil, 27 rue Jacob, 75006 Paris. Copyright © Editions de l'Olivier/Editions du Seuil, 1995. Translation copyright © Ros Schwartz, 1999

Virginie Despentes

Fuck Me is taken from the novel *Baise-moi*. Published by kind permission of Editions Florent-Massot, 20 rue des Petits Champs, 75002, Paris. Copyright © Virginie Despentes, 1996. Translation copyright © Boris Belay, 1999

Tonino Benacquista

The Bad Boys' Garden is taken from the collection *La machine à broyer les petites filles*. Published by kind permission of Editions Payot & Rivages, 106 Boulevard St Germain, 75006 Paris. Copyright © Editions Payot & Rivages, 1993. Translation copyright © Steve Cox, 1999

Michel Houellebecq

The Port of Call is taken from the novel *Whatever*. Published by kind permission of Serpent's Tail, 4 Blackstock Mews, London N4 2BT. *Whatever* was originally published in French by Maurice Nadeau under the title *Extension du domaine de la lutte*.

Copyright Details

Copyright © Maurice Nadeau, 1994. Translation copyright © Paul Hammond, 1999

Guillaume Dustan

Serge the Beauty & Rendezvous is taken from the novel *In My Room*. Published by kind permission of Serpent's Tail, 4 Blackstock Mews, London N4 2BT. *In My Room* was originally published in French under the title *Dans ma chambre*. Copyright © P.O.L. éditeur, 1996. Translation copyright © Brad Rumph, 1998

Agnès Desarthe

Transient Bliss is taken from the novel *Quelques minutes de bonheur absolu*. Published by kind permission of Editions du Seuil, 27 rue Jacob, 75006 Paris. Copyright © Editions de l'Olivier/Editions du Seuil, 1993. Translation copyright © Ros Schwartz, 1999

Lorette Nobécourt

Irritation is taken from the novel *La démangeaison*. Published by kind permission of Société d'Edition Les Belles Lettres, 95 Boulevard Raspail, 75006 Paris. Copyright © Lorette Nobécourt, 1994. Translation copyright © Boris Belay, 1999

Copyright Details

Mehdi Belhaj Kacem

Anteform is taken from the novel *L'Antéforme*. Published by kind permission of Editions Tristram, B.P. 110, 32002 Auch cedex. Copyright © Editions Tristram 1997. Translation copyright © Boris Belay, 1999

Frédéric Beigbeder

Trashed is taken from the novel *Vacances dans le coma*. Published by kind permission of the author and Editions Grasset & Fasquelle, 61 rue des Saints-Pères, 75006 Paris. Copyright © Editions Grasset & Fasquelle, 1994. Translation copyright © Christine Donougher, 1999

Eric Faye

Dinner with the Zeuses is taken from the collection of short stories *Le mystère des trois frontières*. Published by kind permission of Le Serpent à Plumes, 20 rue des Petits Champs, 75002 Paris. Copyright © Le Serpent à Plumes, 1998. Translation copyright © Steve Cox, 1999

Vincent Ravalec

Black-Magic Nostalgia is taken from the novel *Nostalgie de la magie noire*. Published by kind permission of Editions Flammarion, 26 rue Racine, 75006 Paris. Copyright © Editions Flammarion, 1998. Translation copyright © Will Hobson, 1999

Copyright Details

Ilan Duran Cohen

Wonderland is taken from the novel *Chronique Alicienne*. Published by kind permission of Actes Sud, Le Méjan, Place Nina-Berberova, Arles 13200 & 18 rue Séguier, 75006 Paris. Copyright © Actes Sud, 1997. Translation copyright © Will Hobson, 1999

Abdourahman Waberi

The Gallery of the Insane is taken from the collection *Le pays sans ombre*. Published by kind permission of Le Serpent à Plumes, 20 rue des Petits Champs, 75002 Paris. Copyright © Le Serpent à Plumes, 1994. Translation copyright © Michael Dash, 1999

Mounsi

Into the Void is taken from the novel *La noce des fous*. Published by kind permission of Editions Stock, 27 rue Cassette, 75006 Paris. Copyright © Editions Stock, 1990. Translation copyright © Michael Dash, 1999

Mathieu Lindon

F. N. Rally is taken from the novel *Le procès de Jean-Marie Le Pen*. Published by kind permission of P.O.L., 33 rue Saint-André-des-Arts, 75006 Paris. Copyright © P.O.L. éditeur, 1998. Translation copyright © William Rodarmor, 1999

Copyright Details

Marcel Möring

In Babylon

(translated from the Dutch by Stacey Knecht)

'Marcel Möring is beyond doubt one of the most imaginative and perceptive novelists writing today.'

PAUL BINDING, TLS

The worst blizzard the East Netherlands has seen in many years has left Nathan Hollander and his niece, Nina, snowbound in the deserted house of their late Uncle Herman. Waiting for the storm to subside, they piece together the story of their forefathers, a family of itinerant clockmakers who came from Eastern Europe to the Netherlands in the seventeenth century and fled to America in 1939.

In this funny, quirky epic novel, Marcel Möring weaves a gloriously inventive and very human story about man's constant drive towards progression and expansion, his coming and going, from the Old World to the New – and his desire, despite everything, for home and homeland.

'Certain books make the reader recall what extraordinary contraptions these objects are. Paper, some glue, ink: lo and behold, a Tardis. Not much to look at from the outside, but inside, infinite, forever unfolding, a tower to the clouds and a tunnel deep into the earth, an arrow into the heart. *In Babylon* is such a book. It is impossible to put this fat, rich novel into any kind of category. It moves confidently between family history, fairy story, love story, ghost story. Like the Jewish family whose stories it unfolds, it is wide-ranging, adaptable, learned and clever.'

ERICA WAGNER, The Times

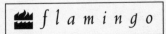

Geneviève Jurgensen

The Disappearance

(translated from the French by Adriana Hunter)

'Heart-rending. An impressively simple book, beautifully translated, it will surely become a classic of the genre – a literary answer to the pain of loss.' ROBERT MCCRUM, *Observer*

'Every parent's ultimate nightmare is the prospect of something happening to their children. It happened to Geneviève. One night in 1980, her sister-in-law collected her seven and four-year-old daughters from Paris to drive them to her in-laws. They never got there. Both children were killed in a terrible accident and somehow she has managed to describe the aftermath in this heart-rending collection of letters to a friend. I could hardly see the words of this beautiful, lucid and intelligent book through my tears.'

KATE FIGES, *Woman's Journal*

'Enlightening, sympathetic and intelligent, *The Disappearance* shows us not only how the unbearable can be borne, but also that to relieve one's suffering by writing does not diminish love.' KATIE CAMPBELL, *Evening Standard*

'The most affecting stories are those rooted in truth where one human heart speaks directly to another. Through her letters – the girls live again: Jurgensen is able to re-create the smell and touch of small children so well it makes you flinch. Shattering and beautiful, *The Disappearance* loses none of its simple power in translation. I found myself holding my breath, tears pricking behind my eyes.'

MARGARETTE DRISCOLL, *Sunday Times*

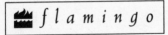 *flamingo*

Nanne Tepper

The Happy
Hunting Grounds

(translated from the Dutch by Sam Garrett)

'A convincing portrayal of an intoxicating relationship and also an unusually honest depiction of adolescent obsession with sexual experimentation.' *Independent on Sunday*

Teenagers Lisa and Victor are closer than a brother and sister have any right to be. So close that they smother and suffocate one another, yanking and wrestling their lives and emotions into a tangled knot. In the flat, damp wooded fen that is their homeland, Lisa and Victor grow into loud, aggressive, foul-mouthed loners who are able to find peace and comfort only when alone together – at school, at home, in bed . . .

Whisky-fuelled, taboo-blind and sharp-tongued, *The Happy Hunting Grounds* is a long, long day's journey into night, an unnervingly compelling tale from the marshy great plains of the northern Netherlands.

'*The Happy Hunting Grounds* is constructed in the form of a symphony, with four distinct movements, each different in style and tempo. It is dense, learned, oblique and allusive (though not intimidatingly so), quoting generously from popular songs and literary works, from Vladimir Nabokov to Barbara Cartland. Tepper binds his material together with admirable artistry. He is a writer of real talent.'

ANDREW BISWELL, *Daily Telegraph*

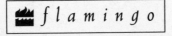 *flamingo*